KING, PHILIP
DARK LUCY. A PLAY. BY PHILIP
KING AND PARNELL BRADBURY.
822.914   -008

Dark Lucy

A Play

by

PHILIP KING
and
PARNELL BRADBURY

SAMUEL  FRENCH

LONDON
NEW YORK   TORONTO   SYDNEY   HOLLYWOOD

© 1971 BY PHILIP KING AND PARNELL BRADBURY

This play is fully protected under the copyright laws of the British Commonwealth of Nations, the United States of America, and all countries of the Berne and Universal Copyright Conventions.

All rights are strictly reserved.

It is an infringement of the copyright to give any public performance or reading of this play either in its entirety or in the form of excerpts without the prior consent of the copyright owners. No part of this publication may be transmitted, stored in a retrieval system, or reproduced in any form or by any means, electronic, mechanical, photocopying, manuscript, typescript, recording, or otherwise, without the prior permission of the copyright owners.

SAMUEL FRENCH LTD, 26 SOUTHAMPTON STREET, STRAND, LONDON WC2, or their authorized agents, issue licences to amateurs to give performances of this play on payment of a fee. **The fee must be paid, and the licence obtained, before a performance is given.**

Licences are issued subject to the understanding that it shall be made clear in all advertising matter that the audience will witness an amateur performance; and that the names of the authors of plays shall be included on all announcements and on all programmes.

The royalty fee indicated below is subject to contract and subject to variation at the sole discretion of Samuel French Ltd.

> Basic fee for each and every
> performance by amateurs   £7
> in the British Isles

In theatres or halls seating 600 or more the fee will be subject to negotiation.

In territories overseas the fee quoted above may not apply. Applications must be made to our local authorized agents, or if there is no such agent, to Samuel French Ltd, London.

Applications for professional productions should be made to ERIC GLASS LTD., 28 Berkeley Square, London W1.

ISBN 0 573 01110 9

MADE AND PRINTED IN GREAT BRITAIN BY
LATIMER TREND AND CO. LTD, PLYMOUTH

MADE IN ENGLAND

DARK LUCY

First presented by the Northampton Repertory Players at the Royal Theatre, Northampton, on the 15th April 1970, with the following cast of characters:

The Reverend Gavin Clevedon	John Bott
Carol Clevedon	Sheila Barker
Dr Thomas Vann	Michael ffoulkes
Mrs Wilson	Elsie Winsor
Lucy Manning	Valerie Georgeson
Edward Hastings	Keith Grenville
Grace Roberts	Beatrix Carter

Directed by Willard Stoker
Settings by Alan Miller Bunford

ACT I
   Scene 1   A room in the Vicarage in a Sussex village. Mid-morning
   Scene 2   The same. An hour later

ACT II   The same, 7.15 that evening

ACT III   The living-room in Dark Lucy's cottage. Ten minutes later

Time - the present

DARK LUCY

ACT I

SCENE 1

A room at the Vicarage. Mid-morning
The room, lounge-cum-study, is pleasantly but simply furnished

When the CURTAIN *rises, Grace Roberts, the daily help, a sensible woman of sixty-five, is discovered alone in the room, dusting the desk. A largish Hoover cleaner is in the centre of the room.*
Gavin Clevedon comes in, carrying a small bag, and a macintosh over his arm. He is a well-built, not too parson-ish man of thirty-eight

Grace (*seeing him*) Oh! You're back already, sir!
Gavin Yes, but—er—carry on with whatever you have to do, Grace. I don't want the room for a while yet.
Grace Had a nice time, sir?
Gavin (*smiling*) I've only been away a day, you know.
Grace Still it was a change. Nice to get away from it all at times.
Gavin I hardly consider taking the usual Sunday services in a strange—and extremely draughty—church "getting away from it all". (*Hesitantly, trying not to show anxiety*) Er—everything—all right?
Grace (*knowing full well what he means; with brightness*) Oh, yes, sir. As a matter of fact, Mrs Clevedon said she had a really good night, last night.

Gavin gives a little sigh of relief

And she certainly had a good breakfast this morning; a proper breakfast, I mean.
Gavin (*quietly*) That's fine.
Grace She's gone out for a bit of a walk.
Gavin Do you know where?
Grace (*dusting the desk*) No, sir. She just said she fancied a walk. But she said she wouldn't be long; went about half an hour ago.
Gavin H'm!
Grace I've practically finished in here now if you do want to stay. Oh, and there's your morning post, and some messages on your pad.
Gavin (*going to the desk*) Thank you, Grace.
Grace (*indicating his bag and macintosh*) Shall I take them up to your room for you?

Gavin No, thanks. You do enough running about. (*He puts the bag and mac down, picks up a small pad and looks at it*)

Grace (*moving to dust the french windows; with a smile*) Are you tellin' me I'm gettin' old, sir?

Gavin (*throwing the pad on the desk*) Nothing there that can't wait. (*To Grace*) What's that? Getting old? You? (*Picking up two or three letters and glancing quickly and casually at the envelopes*) Fiddlesticks!

Grace I am, you know. (*Looking out of the window*) I'm older than that memorial out there in the square.

Gavin You may be older than it is, Grace, but you're in a better state of repair. It's a disgrace to the village.

Grace I can remember when it was first built—fifty-one years ago—the year I left school and—(*she breaks off suddenly*)—oh!

Gavin (*vaguely*) What?

Grace Here's Mrs Clevedon coming back now. (*Anxiously*) Oh dear! I hope she's all right. She looks . . .

Gavin moves quickly to the window, looks out, then immediately opens the window and calls

Gavin (*calling*) Carol! Carol! (*Puzzled*) What on earth's the . . . ? (*Calling again*) Carol! Come in this way.

Grace (*still looking out*) She *is* upset, isn't she?

After a moment's pause, Carol Clevedon appears at the window. She has obviously been running, and is very shaken. She stands just outside the window, puts her two hands to her temples for a moment. Carol is thirty—dark, slight and highly strung

Gavin (*anxiously*) Carol, what . . . ?

Carol (*almost sharply*) I'm all right.

Gavin But . . .

Carol I'm all right, I tell you; or I will be in a minute.

Grace Can I get you a cup of tea or something?

Carol For God's sake, don't fuss.

Gavin (*sharply*) Carol!

Gavin and Grace are almost blocking the entrance to the room

Carol If you'd let me come in, I'd like to sit down for a moment. (*She comes into the room and sits in a chair*)

Grace I'll fetch a cup of tea.

Carol Don't bother.

Grace I have some made.

Grace goes off quickly, taking the Hoover

Carol (*almost between her teeth*) I don't want any damned tea.

Gavin stands looking at her for a moment, then moves away. He stands by the desk, with his back to Carol, idly picking up a paper knife. Carol, at last, turns and realizes Gavin is not going to ask her anything—that he is hurt

(*At last; reluctantly*) I've had an awful shock.

Gavin turns facing her

(*Almost angrily*) I *have*, Gavin. I'm not just putting on an act. I *have*, I tell you.

Gavin (*quietly*) Am I disputing it?

Carol (*seething; quietly*) Oh God!

Grace enters carrying a cup of tea

Grace (*brightly*) Here we are! (*She holds the cup out towards Carol*)

Carol (*restraining herself with an effort; indicating the table*) Put it down there, Grace—please.

Grace But . . . (*Seeing the angry look in Carol's eyes, she puts the tea on the table, then moves to go out*)

Carol (*calling sharply*) Grace!

Grace moves back

(*After a pause*) Do you know the old woman who lives in that tumbledown cottage in River Lane?

Grace D'you mean "Dark Lucy"?

Carol "Dark . . . ?" Well, if that's her name, yes, I do. Is that what she's called—"Dark Lucy"? "Foul" would be more appropriate. *Do* you know her?

Grace I know her as someone to keep away from, that's all. Have you seen her this morning, then?

Carol (*quietly*) Yes, I have.

Grace Close to?

Carol Yes. The first time. I've passed her place often—I like that walk down to the river—but I've never seen her around.

Gavin But, what *about*—old Lucy?

Carol (*sharply*) Do *you* know her?

Gavin No. She's a difficult person to get to know. I've tried calling on her once or twice, but . . .

Grace She never let you into her cottage, did she, sir?

Gavin No, she didn't. Wouldn't even answer the door; although I knew she was in each time I called.

Grace Never let's anybody in; never has, not as long as I can remember. 'Expect she's scared of anyone seein' the state the place must be in; specially someone like you—in authority, so to speak; someone who might be able to do something about her—and it's about time somebody did.

Carol It certainly is.

Grace The place is an eyesore—falling to pieces, and goodness knows when it saw any paint last.

Gavin (*to Carol*) But what . . . ? (*With a little laugh*) Don't tell me that—old Lucy gave you your—awful shock.

Carol (*angrily*) You *do* think I'm putting on an act, don't you?

Gavin (*very conscious of Grace*) Carol!

Grace Give anybody a shock, Dark Lucy. But it's a shame you should've been frightened—your nerves in the state they are just now.

Carol and Gavin exchange quick glances; Carol's angry; Gavin's apprehensive

Carol (*in a deliberately controlled voice*) Yes—well . . . All right, Grace. Don't let me stop you from getting on with whatever you have to do.

Grace I was just going to turn out the dining-room.

Carol I'll be in to give you a hand in a few minutes.

Grace Don't you hurry, Mrs Clevedon. And don't forget your tea; do you good.

Grace exits

Carol (*muttering*) For—God's sake . . . ! (*She rises, picks up the cup of tea, moves to the window and deliberately throws the tea out on the lawn*)

Gavin watches this silently. Carol puts the cup back in the saucer. She looks defiantly at Gavin, who says nothing

I feel better for that!

Gavin (*quietly*) Good.

Carol Why don't you say what you're really thinking?

Gavin Why don't you tell me what's upset you—this time?

Carol is about to take him up on the "this time", but checks herself

Carol That damned old woman in River Lane—she frightened the life out of me, that's what.

Gavin (*patiently*) But surely—just *seeing* her . . .

Carol It wasn't a case of just *seeing* her. (*After a pause*) I was coming back up River Lane just now—and as I was passing her cottage her gate was open—I've never seen it open before—and I could see the marvellous display of flowers in her front garden. How anyone can tend a garden as she must do, and yet let the house itself get into the filthy state it's in . . .

Gavin You didn't go into the house, surely?

Carol (*snapping*) Of course I didn't. But I've got eyes, haven't I? I could see the windows—and the rags hanging at them. I don't suppose either have been washed for years. Absolutely disgusting! But the garden—I was so staggered by it—I—I—didn't realize what I was doing, I suppose, but I went through the gate, right into it.

Gavin (*quietly*) You shouldn't have done that.

Carol I've *told* you—I did it without realizing. I just stood there, as I say, staggered. Then—I suddenly knew there was someone standing close to me. I turned round quickly, and—there was that disgusting-looking old crone, right at my side. It was all I could do to stop myself screaming out with fright. I hadn't heard her moving—she was just there—right by me. (*She shudders*) Pah!

Gavin What did she say—do?

Carol That was the awful part of it. She didn't say anything—not then. Just stood, staring at me, as if I were . . .

Gavin (*after a slight pause*) As if you were what?

Carol Well, if I'd been something from outer space she couldn't've stared more.

Gavin Didn't you speak to her—apologize for trespassing?

Carol When I was capable of speech, yes. But I don't think she was even listening to me—just went on staring, until—until I said something about her display of flowers being the most beautiful I'd ever seen. Then she—she seemed to—I don't know how to explain, quite. Her eyes—lit up, and she said in a funny, choked voice, "Yes, they are beautiful, but—not as beautiful as you."

Gavin (*incredulously*) What?

Carol And then was when it happened. She . . . (*She shudders*) Oh, God! The filthy old creature suddenly put her arms round me . . .

Gavin Carol!

Carol She did, I tell you.

Gavin (*anxiously*) Darling—you don't mean she—attacked you?

Carol *Attacked?* (*After a slight pause*) She tried to get hold of me. I thought I should be sick on the spot. I was afraid I was going to faint but I managed to push her off, and I got away as fast as I could.

Gavin Darling, you didn't push her over, I hope? An old woman like that, she might . . .

Carol (*with exasperation*) For Heaven's sake . . . ! I didn't stop to see what I'd done. I just wanted to get away. I felt—ugh!—unclean . . .

Gavin Yes, I can understand—it must have been rather unpleasant . . .

Carol "Rather unpleasant"! That, Gavin, is a masterpiece of understatement, even for you. (*Excitedly*) I tell you . . .

Gavin (*with patience*) Carol, please, don't get yourself so worked up about—about what really amounts to nothing at all.

Carol is about to burst forth. Gavin goes on quickly

I'm sure the old woman meant no harm. Can't you see—it might've been just the fact that you'd taken the trouble to go in and look at her garden, and that you admired her flowers, and said so. God knows, there can't be many people who even pass the time of day with her, let alone . . . Her embracing you—it could only have been an impulsive gesture of gratitude.

Carol (*after the slightest pause*) It wasn't like that.

Gavin But . . .

Carol (*almost under her breath*) It wasn't like that, I tell you.

Gavin looks at her steadily for a moment, or two, then with a sigh, moves to the desk

Gavin (*after a pause; quietly*) When do you see the doctor again?
Carol Tomorrow. (*Rising; sharply*) Why? For God's sake! You don't think I'm having hallucinations now, do you? (*Brokenly*) Oh—God ... ! (*She suddenly breaks down and begins to sob*)
Gavin (*coming to her quickly; speaking firmly*) Carol!
Carol (*moving quickly and slightly away*) Leave me alone, please.
Gavin (*taking her by the shoulders*) Carol! Carol! Stop it! Please stop it! Try to get a grip on yourself!
Carol (*slightly hysterical*) Why won't you ever take my word for anything.
Gavin Carol!
Carol I'm not mental! I'm not! I'm not!
Gavin Nobody has ever suggested that you are.
Carol You think I'm making all this up—about that old woman, don't you?
Gavin (*with some firmness*) Carol, sit down again.
Carol No!
Gavin Carol!

Carol moves slowly to an armchair and sits

(*Moving near her*) Now ...
Carol (*brokenly*) Gavin—please—please don't bully me. (*She covers her face with her hands and cries*)
Gavin (*putting his hand to his head*) I'm not going to ...
Carol (*still crying*) Please—let me cry. Dr Vann said—he told me—when I felt as I do now—it was good for me to cry. It relieves the tension. (*She covers her face with her hands again. Occasionally she dabs her eyes with a handkerchief*)

Gavin squats on his haunches beside her

(*After a slight pause; pulling herself together a little*) Damn that old woman!
Gavin Carol, listen. (*Hurriedly*) And I'm not bullying you—believe me I'm not—but, you know, you are making a very large mountain out of a very small molehill.
Carol (*excitedly*) But she did put her arms round me.
Gavin (*quickly, but patiently*) I'm not saying she didn't. What I'm trying to make you see is—if you were calmer you'd realize she meant no harm by it.
Carol (*after a slight pause*) I suppose you're right.
Gavin I know I am.
Carol It must be wonderful to be so self-assured.

Gavin is silent

(*After a slight pause*) Am I ever going to get better—really right again?
Gavin Of course you are.
Carol Not while we stay in this damned village, I'm not.

Gavin rises slowly, a strained, hurt look on his face. He moves to the window, running a hand wearily across his brow as he does so

Can't we get away from it?

Act I, Scene 1

Gavin (*wearily*) We've been over this so often.
Carol (*flaring up*) Then let's go over it again! Doesn't my health mean anything to you?
Gavin (*after looking at her for a moment*) If only I knew—for certain . . .
Carol Knew what? Whether I'm really ill, or just putting on an act?
Gavin Whether . . .
Carol If you can't see for yourself, why don't you ask the doctor? He'd tell you how ill I am.
Gavin (*with some firmness*) Carol, will you *listen* to me.
Carol (*almost overlapping*) You think that because I used to be on the stage . . .
Gavin (*topping her*) Carol! (*After a slight pause*) Of course I know you're —not well. But will—leaving here—make you any better? Remember, it was for your sake we left Birmingham, and . . .
Carol Birmingham! I loathed the place; always did. Even when I went there on tour. I hated it. But to expect me to live my life there indefinitely . . .
Gavin You're not living there now, so . . . (*He waves a hand, dismissing "Birmingham"*) But I would ask you to remember that before I took this living, I brought you here—you saw the place—you said you were willing to come here. And now . . . before we've been here three months . . .
Carol I made a mistake. Lots of people do. We're not all infallible, like you.
Gavin But you surely can't expect me to give up living after living so that you can go on searching for your—your "Shangri-la". If only you'd help me begin to create it.
Carol It's no use, Gavin. I can't live up to these high ideals of yours. (*After a slight pause*) I suppose that's the trouble really. I was never cut out to be a parson's wife.
Gavin You haven't tried—not very hard, have you?
Carol No. Because I know it would be hopeless. I can't mix with your —your parochial set. I'm not saying there's anything wrong with them, but—I just don't talk their language. And as for—Women's Institutes —Coffee Mornings—Jumble Sales . . . Much of those and I *would* end up in a mental home.

Gavin stands with his back to her at the window

(*After a slight pause*) And let's face it; I'm not exactly in the "top ten" as far as popularity goes in this village, am I?
Gavin You can't blame the villagers for that, can you? If you gave them a chance to—really know you . . .
Carol (*with an abrupt laugh*) They'd like me a damn' sight less. (*Quietly*) You should never have married me, Gavin.
Gavin (*still looking out of the window*) You mean—I shouldn't have fallen in love with you?
Carol (*after a look towards him*) Yes.
Gavin But I did, didn't I?

Carol (*moving towards him; quietly*) But are you—and be honest with me—are you still in love with me—in spite of . . . ?
Gavin (*turning to face her*) Yes, I am. (*With a little smile*) In spite of . . .
Carol (*with a catch in her voice*) Oh, Gavin . . .
Gavin But what about you?
Carol (*after a slight pause*) I love you—but I'm scared.
Gavin Scared of what?
Carol Losing you. (*Quickly*) Oh, I don't mean to another woman—but—your job. I'm scared that—if I can't go along with you in that, I shall be—left behind.
Gavin (*quietly*) When you're feeling better . . .
Carol (*suddenly rushing into his arms*) Oh, my darling! (*She cannot go on for a moment*) You—you make me feel such a swine. Gavin—Gavin, my dear, I will try—I will try to get some sort of grip on myself, and be a help to you.
Gavin If only you could—*would*.
Carol I'll try, I promise. And you forgive me for being so beastly to you—just now.
Gavin (*quietly*) Carol . . .
Carol (*moving away*) It was that foul old woman's fault. If she hadn't upset me—terrified me . . .
Gavin Carol, please, forget all about—poor Lucy.
Carol (*almost returning to her old self*) Forget . . . ? (*With a little moan of exasperation*) It's so easy for you to say that. Forget—*and* forgive, I suppose? That's part of your stock-in-trade, isn't it? But it isn't easy for *me*. Gavin, that woman's going to haunt me. I know she is. There's something evil about her.
Gavin (*strongly*) Carol, I'm going to be firm with you about this; for your own sake I've got to be, otherwise this trivial incident—yes, I *mean that*—this trivial incident will become an obsession with you, and heaven knows what . . . (*He breaks off suddenly*) Now, listen to me. After lunch, you and I are going down to Lucy's place . . .
Carol (*loudly*) No!
Gavin We're going down there together—we'll see her—talk to her.
Carol I won't! I won't go! (*Near hysteria again*) Do you *want* me to go out of my mind? Is that what you're really aiming at?
Gavin Carol!
Carol After what I've just been through—to ask me to go through it again . . . !
Gavin Don't you see—it's for your own good? You've got to rid yourself of this—this utterly stupid obsession.
Carol (*brokenly*) Oh, God! Oh, God!
Gavin I know the woman's odd, eccentric, but saying she is evil . . .
Carol You heard what Grace said about her, didn't you?
Gavin (*trying to be patient*) All Grace said was . . .

Carol, not listening, rushes to the door and calls loudly

Carol Grace! Grace! Come in here a minute!

Act I, Scene 1

Gavin Carol, for heaven's sake . . . !
Carol (*calling louder*) Grace!
Grace (*off*) I'm coming, Mrs Clevedon.
Gavin (*moving to Carol and taking her wrist*) Carol, for pity's sake stop all this, do you hear?
Carol (*hysterically, struggling to free herself*) Let me go! Let me go! (*Calling again*) Grace!

Grace appears in the doorway

Grace I'm sorry, I was at the far end of the dining-room and . . . (*She pulls up—seeing Gavin and Carol struggling*) Oh! Oh, dear! What . . . ?
Gavin (*hardly realizing what he is saying*) It's all right, Grace. It's all right!
Grace (*bewildered*) But . . .
Carol (*loudly*) Grace, what was it you said just now about that old woman?
Grace (*still bewildered*) What . . . ?
Carol (*vehemently*) That old hag in River Lane.
Gavin Carol, you mustn't . . .
Carol (*overlapping*) What was it you said, Grace?
Grace (*flustered*) Well—I can't remember, not off-hand.
Carol You said you knew her as someone to keep away from, didn't you?
Grace Yes, that's right. I did, but . . .
Carol Why did you say that?
Grace Why? Well . . .
Carol Why did you say it?
Grace Well—I mean to say, you've only to look at her, haven't you?
Carol But you meant more than that—her looks. You meant she was evil, didn't you?
Grace (*quickly*) Oh, no, mum. I never said that.
Gavin (*also quickly*) Of course you didn't, Grace.
Carol (*overlapping; to Grace*) But you *meant* it, didn't you?
Gavin Stop badgering Grace.
Carol (*almost overlapping*) She *is* evil, isn't she?
Grace Well, I can't rightly—I know she's "funny", but . . .
Carol But why did you say something ought to be done about her?
Gavin (*strongly*) Carol, once and for all, stop this.
Carol (*after a slight pause; more quietly*) You're quite right, Grace. Something ought to be done about her, and—(*looking at Gavin*)—if my husband won't use whatever influence he's supposed to have—I'll find someone who will. (*She gives a shudder of repulsion. Almost muttering*) I'm going to try and lie down for a while.

Carol looks at Gavin for a moment, then goes quickly out

Gavin, after a moment, moves wearily to the window and stands looking out

Grace (*quietly, sympathetically*) I'm sorry, sir. (*After a slight pause*) And I thought earlier on, she seemed so much better. I *am* sorry.

Gavin (*quietly*) I'm sorry, too, Grace; sorry you've been subjected to . . .
Grace Don't you worry about me. You've got enough to put up with. I'll go and finish off in the dining-room. (*She moves to go*)
Gavin (*turning*) Grace . . .
Grace Yes, sir?
Gavin Please—sit down a moment, will you?

Grace moves to an upright chair and sits

(*Moving to his desk*) Tell me what you know about—about Dark Lucy—that is the name you say she's known by?
Grace Yes, sir.
Gavin What's her real name?
Grace (*after a moment's thought*) Good Lord! That's funny, isn't it? I can't tell you, sir. I suppose I must've heard it some time or other, but nobody ever speaks of her except as Dark Lucy.
Gavin Is she married? I mean is she a widow, or . . .
Grace I don't know whether she ever has had a husband. Not so far as I know she hasn't. (*After a slight pause*) It's funny, really, but I don't know much—anything about her at all.
Gavin Please don't think I'm taking what my wife said about her seriously. In her present state of health she *is* apt to exaggerate the most trivial incident. Had she been in her normal state of mind, she would never have said what she did about the poor woman.
Grace No, of course not. But what happened to make her say it? Had Lucy been shouting at her? She does do that sometimes.
Gavin (*quickly*) No, no! All she did was . . . (*He pulls up abruptly*) Oh, it was nothing, really. (*Quickly*) Has she always lived alone in that cottage?
Grace Ever since I've known her.
Gavin But she has—no-one—no relations—friends?
Grace I've never heard of relations. And as for her friends, I can't imagine anyone wanting to be friendly with her—even if she gave 'em the chance, which she doesn't.
Gavin (*to himself*) Poor soul! And you know nothing whatever about her—her past—nothing?
Grace No, sir. No, she's just one of those oddities that most villages seem to have in some form or other, and everyone seems to sort of take her for granted. You see her now and then and think nothing of it and sometimes weeks go by and you don't see her at all and forget all about her; sometimes the kiddies torment her—them that aren't scared of her, that is.
Gavin H'm!
Grace When I was a kiddie my mother always said I wasn't to torment her or go near her. (*She smiles*) 'Cos she was a witch, Mother said.
Gavin (*incredulously*) A witch?
Grace (*with a little laugh*) 'Course, people were more superstitious then than they are now.
Gavin Yes, I suppose . . . (*He pulls up suddenly, struck by what Grace has just said. He stands quite still; puzzled and disturbed. Quietly*) Grace . . .
Grace (*placidly*) Yes, sir?

Act I, Scene 1

Gavin You say—your *mother*—used to warn you about "Dark Lucy"—when you were a child?
Grace That's right, sir, she did. Used to threaten my brother and me with her. The times she said, "If you don't behave I'll fetch 'Dark Lucy' to you." And that used to quieten us down, I can tell you.
Gavin (*staring at her*) But—Grace . . .
Grace Yes, sir?

Gavin is reluctant to speak for a moment. He moves away, very disturbed

Gavin (*at last; quietly but pointedly*) Er, what was she—like—in those days?
Grace Like? "Dark Lucy"? Well, much as she is now; dirty and . . .
Gavin (*quickly*) But—younger, of course.
Grace (*placidly*) Well, she must've been, mustn't she? But she didn't look it. (*Innocently*) Funny, now you come to mention it. She doesn't seem to have changed at all; not in all the years I've known her, and I'm—what now?—sixty-five. (*She pulls up with a little jerk*) Oh, but . . . ! (*Puzzled*) But that can't be right, can it, sir?
Gavin You mean—you're not sixty-five?
Grace (*now very disturbed*) Oh, yes, I'm sixty-five all right—last February, but—(*almost in awe*)—her—"Dark Lucy"—she was—she *seemed*—(*with conviction*)—no, she *was*—she *was*—she was an *old woman* when I was going to school—over fifty years ago, so . . . ! (*She looks towards Gavin wide-eyed. In an awed whisper*) Dear God! Whatever age must she be now? Why—she must be . . . ! No! No! It isn't possible. And yet . . . ! (*Rather frightened*) Oh, sir . . . !
Gavin (*quietly*) Grace, Grace, don't upset yourself. Just think back—carefully. Are you sure that Lucy was an old woman when you were a child? You know, when we're *very* young we're inclined to think anyone over thirty is senile.
Grace (*almost excitedly*) She was, sir, I'll swear to it. And there's others in the village who would, too! There's Mollie Benson—Mollie Farrow that was—who went to school with me—you ask *her*.
Gavin (*almost sharply*) No, Grace. We won't ask Mrs Benson. It's better that we don't ask anybody—anything. (*He goes to the window*)
Grace But . . . (*She looks towards Gavin's back for a moment*) Are you—frightened of something, sir?
Gavin (*uneasily*) Frightened?
Grace Well, if "Dark Lucy" is—and she *must* be—well into her hundreds—she must be—*well* into them—well there is something—frightening about it, isn't there? Something—uncanny. I mean—her, as active as she is—tending that garden of hers like she does . . . It isn't human, is it? (*With a sudden thought*) Oh, no!
Gavin What is it, Grace?
Grace (*in a frightened voice*) Oh, sir, you don't think it's possible that my mother was right—that—"Dark Lucy" *is*—a witch?
Gavin (*fairly sharply*) Grace, you mustn't say things like that, or even think them. There must be some perfectly rational explanation.
Grace But there must be something—not *right* about her, sir. Ordinary

folk don't live to that age; and if they do—they don't get about—work like she can. There must be something—unnatural about her. You can't get away from it.

Gavin (*firmly, but troubled*) Grace, I'm going to ask you not to say anything to anybody—*anybody*—about Lucy's age. Will you promise me you won't?

Grace But . . .

Gavin As I've just said, there must be a rational explanation. We don't want to stir up trouble for that poor woman, do we?

Grace Trouble?

Gavin Say she is—it's ridiculous even to think it—but say she *is* the age you say she must be, and it gets around the village? What's going to happen? Sooner or later the press will get on to it, and, before we know where we are, we shall have reporters—television people down here, all hounding that poor woman—prying into her past. And we don't know, do we, what turned her into the eccentric she is? They'll probe and probe. Grace, we can't let that happen to her. We can't. You will promise me that you won't say anything to anyone?

Grace Well, of course, sir, if you think it for the best.

Gavin Believe me, it is.

Grace Don't worry, sir. I won't say nothing to nobody.

Gavin (*after giving her a little "thank you" pat on the shoulder*) And, in the meantime, I'll try to . . . (*He suddenly thinks of something*) You don't know, I suppose, if she was born here in this village?

Grace No, sir, I don't.

Gavin And you can't remember her proper name?

Grace No, I can't. But I'm sure if I asked some of the older folk . . .

Gavin No, don't do that. It's too risky. The less she is brought to people's attention the better. But I was wondering if there was any record of her in the church . . .

The telephone rings. Gavin answers it

(*Into the phone*) The Vicarage. The vicar here . . . Oh, yes, Nurse? . . . (*Quietly*) I see . . . Yes, yes, of course. I'll come along at once . . . Thank you, Nurse . . . 'Bye. (*He replaces the receiver and turns to Grace. Quietly*) Old Mrs Robinson in Church Street.

Grace Oh, dear! Is she . . . ?

Gavin That was the nurse looking after her. She says she think it's near the end.

Grace Oh, the poor soul! Now *she* could've told you about "Dark Lucy". She's over ninety herself, and . . .

Gavin I'm afraid it's too late to ask her anything now. (*Moving to the bag which he brought in with him*) I'd better get round there right away. (*He takes a Bible and Prayer Book from the bag*) Tell Mrs Clevedon where I've gone if she comes down before I'm back, will you?

Grace Yes, sir.

Gavin (*moving to the door, then turning*) And remember, not a word about —Lucy—especially to my wife.

Act I, Scene 1

Grace Oh, I wouldn't dream of . . .
Gavin Thank you, Grace.

Gavin goes out

Grace stands in troubled thought for a while. Then she gives a little shudder, and her hand moves to the base of her neck. She pulls herself together, notices the cup and saucer, picks them up and moves towards the door

Carol comes into the doorway

Grace (*with a little startled cry*) Oh!
Carol What is it? What's the matter?
Grace Oh, nothing, mum. You startled me, that's all. I thought you were upstairs.
Carol (*moving into the room*) It was no use. I couldn't rest. Where's the Vicar?
Grace He had to go out. He was phoned for. Old Mrs Robinson . . .
Carol (*not really listening*) I see. Can you manage without my help this morning?
Grace Yes, of course. Don't you worry yourself.
Carol I'll just sit down in here for a while.
Grace Yes, you do that.
Carol I hope I didn't—upset you just now, Grace?
Grace (*with "cheeriness"*) No, mum, of course you didn't. Now you'll be all right?
Carol (*with some asperity*) Of course. Why shouldn't I be?

Grace does not reply, but goes out, gently closing the door behind her

Carol stands for a moment or two, then moves listlessly and aimlessly around the room. Finally she moves to the fireplace and stands with her arms stretched out and her hands on the mantelpiece, gazing absently at the empty grate. After quite a pause she suddenly stiffens, as if she has sensed that someone is near. She spins round quickly and gives a little scream, then unconsciously she begins to move towards the window. As she reaches the centre of the room she stops

The shadow of an old woman falls on the path outside the window

Carol (*in a voice choked with horror*) Go away! Go away!

A shadowed hand is extended, as if offering a bunch of flowers

(*Backing a little, and swaying*) No! No! Go away! Go . . .
Carol sways, then suddenly collapses to the floor in a dead faint, as—

the CURTAIN *falls quickly*

Scene 2

An hour later

When the Curtain *rises, Gavin is pacing slowly up and down the room in troubled thought. After a little while, he stands still for a moment, then, as a thought strikes him, he moves to the closed french windows, opens them wide, steps outside, and looks out and around near the window. He then stands on the threshold, looking into the room. Eventually, he shakes his head slowly, then returns into the room, leaving the windows open. He listens intently for a moment, with eyes on the door. He then moves quickly to the door, opens it and speaks off*

Gavin (*eagerly*) I thought I heard you coming down the stairs. Do come in——

Dr Thomas Vann comes into the doorway, carrying his doctor's bag. He is a man of sixty or so, ruddy-faced and wearing well-worn tweeds

—that is, if you can spare me a few minutes.
Doctor (*grinning*) I can't, of course, but I will. (*He moves in*)
Gavin Thank you. (*After closing the door*) Well, Doctor, how is she?
Doctor (*who is a bit of a wag*) I suppose you'd pass out if I said, "Mother and twins all doing well"?
Gavin (*gaping at him*) What?
Doctor Hold your horses! I'm not going to say that. How is she? (*He shrugs his shoulders*) She's all right, at the moment. I've managed to calm her down a bit—a lot in fact.
Gavin Is she sleeping?
Doctor No, no. Resting. I'd rather she slept at night. I've just given her a mild sedative. (*With a smile*) Cheer up. I don't think you'll have any more trouble today.
Gavin (*with a sigh of relief*) Well, I suppose that's *something*. (*Suddenly*) By the way, can I offer you a drink?
Doctor (*putting down his bag; hesitantly*) Er—if I've got my . . . (*He pats his waistcoat pocket*) Ah, yes! I have! So you can! (*He produces a tiny bottle of perfume from his waistcoat pocket*)
Gavin (*blinking at the bottle*) What . . . ?
Doctor (*practically*) Eau-de-Cologne.
Gavin Eau-de . . . ?
Doctor (*with a laugh*) Old professional trick, this. Wouldn't do to call on a patient smelling of drink, so, when I've had—er—whatever you're going to offer me, I shall just rub a little of this over my lips, and Bob's your uncle.
Gavin (*with a rather wan smile*) Whiskey? (*He moves to the cupboard, and searches for a bottle*)
Doctor (*with a grin*) What? In these days? I'm obviously in the wrong

Act I, Scene 2   15

profession. Thanks very much. And since I'm on the slippery slope, I may as well . . . D'you *mind* if I smoke a pipe?

Gavin (*pouring whiskey*) Please do. Soda?

Doctor Thank you. (*He finds his pipe and lights it*)

Gavin Do sit down, please. Carol—talked to you? I'll put it down here. (*He puts the drink on a small table by the Doctor's chair*)

Doctor Thanks. Oh yes—she talked.

Gavin About—Dark Lucy?

Doctor (*after blowing out his match*) Huh-huh!

Gavin (*holding out an ashtray*) About—thinking she saw her here at this window?

Doctor (*after dropping the match in the ashtray*) There doesn't seem to be any doubt in your wife's mind. She's *convinced* she saw her.

Gavin (*slight pause*) Er—what do you think?

Doctor (*raising his glass*) Good health! (*After drinking*) What do *I* think? I didn't bother your wife with lots of questions just now. My chief concern was to calm her down. I'll talk to her later. So, for the moment, I'm reserving judgement.

Gavin looks at him anxiously

(*Aware of Gavin's look*) Can I be very frank with you?

Gavin (*quickly*) Of course.

Doctor (*with a little grin*) I'm always a bit wary when anyone says that to *me*.

Gavin (*slight pause*) Please, go on.

Doctor When your wife first came to me—how long ago was that now? Seven—eight weeks?

Gavin About that.

Doctor Well, I thought then—and right up to today, that she was just an over-emotional woman who was suffering from—some nostalgia. And knowing that she had been an actress before you married her, I couldn't help feeling—unfairly perhaps—that she was—dramatizing her condition—playing a part—to a certain extent *enjoying* a new role—that of an invalid. Does that make sense to you?

Gavin (*quietly*) I've reproached myself so often for thinking what you've just said. . .

The Doctor looks at him keenly

Doctor You have?

Gavin Yes.

Doctor You've never actually spoken to her about it—accused her?

Gavin No. Because I didn't know—for sure.

Doctor No. (*With a little sigh*) It isn't always easy to be sure.

Gavin You spoke of—some nostalgia. I suppose you mean a longing to return to the stage?

Doctor (*after a pause*) I think it goes deeper than that.

Gavin looks at him quizzically

You've *seen* her on the stage, of course?
Gavin (*quietly*) Yes.
Doctor What sort of roles did she take? Dramatic ones, I imagine.
Gavin (*still quietly*) She preferred dramatic parts, certainly.
Doctor (*after a fairly long pause during which he makes a pretence of examining the bowl of his pipe*) Was she—good in them?
Gavin (*after a slight pause*) I would say she was—*capable*.
Doctor Capable. Nothing more?
Gavin I never saw her give a bad performance, but . . .
Doctor But you never saw her—reach the heights?
Gavin No. I don't think Carol has got—what I believe is called—"star quality".
Doctor H'm! (*After a slight pause*) I don't need to tell you I'm not a psychiatrist—I'm just a country G.P.—but I can't help feeling that *that* might be the basic cause of her—trouble. (*He goes on quickly*) Your wife is an intelligent woman, and though she might try to fool others, she couldn't easily fool herself. It *could be* that she knows she hasn't got this—what did you call it?—"star quality", and the knowledge that she could never really succeed in her chosen profession, is the—the canker that's eating into her mind and causing the disturbances.

Gavin moves slowly to the fireplace and stands facing it

(*After a pause; quietly*) And perhaps she sees herself faced with—a second failure.

Gavin turns and looks at the Doctor

I rather gather she isn't finding it easy—adapting herself to the life here, and she has the idea that the local people dislike her. She may have got it into her head that she's letting *you* down now, because she can't adapt herself to being the parson's wife.
Gavin She has hinted as much, certainly, but . . . (*Suddenly*) Doctor, you asked me just now to be frank with you. Now I'm going to ask *you* to be frank with *me*. Is Carol really mentally ill, and if so, what—what's to be done? What chances are there of recovery?
Doctor Good Lord, in this day and age there's no doubt of her recovery —that is, if we can be certain that her only troubles are the ones we've discussed, but—are they? I've got to admit I was very shaken when I realized—(*indicating upstairs with a gesture*)—just now that your wife may be beginning to suffer from—hallucinations.
Gavin You mean—seeing Dark Lucy here?
Doctor If she only imagined she saw her here, yes.
Gavin That may be a sign of a—deeper disturbance?
Doctor It could be. (*After hesitating; firmly*) You see, there are two distinct types of mental disorder. I'm not very well up in this sort of thing, but I can tell you that what the psychiatrists call the "neuroses" can be cured, or at least controlled, but the "psychoses"—when the derangement of the mind is far more serious—well, that's a very different kettle of fish.

Act I, Scene 2

Gavin You mean—it can't be cured?
Doctor (*after a slight pause*) Well—well, not often.
Gavin And—having hallucinations comes under that heading?
Doctor I'm afraid it does. (*After a look at Gavin*) But we don't know—for certain, do we—that it was an hallucination your wife had?
Gavin (*wanting to believe it*) Do you think it at all possible—that the old woman did actually come to that window?
Doctor What I will say is—it can't be ruled out as *im*possible. She's not bedridden, she can walk well enough, but . . .
Gavin But—what?
Doctor It's so utterly—uncharacteristic of her. God knows I've known her all my life—I was born in this village y'know; my father had the practice before me—and I've never—*never* known old Lucy go to anyone's house —never.
Gavin So—you really do think it might have been an—hallucination my wife had?
Doctor Until I know more about what really happened, I'm not going to —I can't—commit myself. Perhaps *someone* did come to the window— perhaps someone vaguely resembling Lucy, but your wife, in the state she was in mentally, couldn't see her as anyone else *but* Lucy. And remember, she admits she fainted within seconds of it happening.
Gavin But isn't it odd that Carol is so definite about the flowers she says Lucy offered her?
Doctor Not if it *was* an hallucination, no. After all, the whole trouble this morning began over flowers, didn't it? They'd be on her mind, in connection with the old woman.
Gavin You don't think, do you, that *that*—this morning's incident—could have been an hallucination too?
Doctor (*firmly*) Oh, no! Far from it! Too—authentic! Your wife described Lucy's garden perfectly. She must have gone into it to do that. And I can *understand* her being—drawn into it, as she says she was. I've always been a keen gardener, and I'm fairly proud of my flower display, but Dark Lucy's beats mine into a cocked hat. The Lord knows how she does it, but *she* manages to grow blooms *I've* never even *seen* in England, let alone grow. No, I think we need have no doubts that your wife did go into that garden. And I can believe Lucy crept up behind her and startled her. The—*embracing* part of it—(*after a shrug*)—I don't think we ought to take that too seriously.
Gavin But Carol *does*. It was the old woman trying to embrace her that frightened her more than anything else. I tried to tell Carol it was a natural reaction to her admiring the garden.
Doctor What did she say to that?
Gavin She said—it wasn't like that at all.
Doctor But what could she have *thought* it was? Not the preliminary to a sexual assault, surely? If Lucy ever *did* have lesbian tendencies, which I very much doubt, they must've died on her years ago. Damn it all, she must be what age now? (*Quite casually*) Good Lord, she must be about . . .

The door opens and Carol, in a quite attractive dressing-gown appears in the doorway

The Doctor breaks off abruptly and rises

Gavin (*also rising, with concern*) Carol!
Doctor (*with assumed jocularity*) Hey! Hey! What's this. I thought I said you were to rest!

Carol is almost unnaturally calm, and her voice is flat

Carol Please sit down again, Doctor.
Doctor But I distinctly told you . . .
Carol (*calmly*) I know. I know exactly what you told me, but—(*with a shrug of the shoulders*)—that has always been one of my—weaknesses—a complete inability to do as I'm told. I was sacked from two jobs because of it. (*After a slight pause*) Please sit down again, Doctor.

The Doctor, with his eyes on Carol, sits

(*To Gavin, indicating his chair*) Gavin . . .

Gavin, after an anxious look towards the Doctor, sits again

(*Seeing the look*) And you needn't look so anxiously at the doctor. I promise I'll behave myself. You've had enough—play-acting—for one day. (*Quickly, as she looks on a table*) Now where are the cigarettes? I don't know why, but Grace always moves them somewhere else when she dusts this room. Ah, here they are! (*She picks up the box from the desk*) Oh, but—am I allowed to smoke, Doctor?
Doctor (*with a grin*) What's the use of my saying anything? You've just told us . . . (*With a nod*) You may smoke.

Carol lights a cigarette from a lighter, then crosses to a chair and sits. Although she is obviously not well, she cannot help "acting", and her technique is excellent. She knows how to say what she has to say, with effect. She also knows the value of a pause

Carol (*after settling herself comfortably*) I hope I haven't interrupted an interesting discussion—about me.
Gavin (*uneasily*) Carol!
Carol (*easily*) Well, you *were* talking about me, surely? I shall feel very slighted if you tell me you were having a heart-to-heart chat about fishing.
Doctor (*aware of Gavin's discomfort; easily*) No, no, Mrs Clevedon. We *were* talking about you.
Carol (*after a slight pause*) And did you come to any—conclusions about me?

Gavin looks uneasily towards the Doctor

Did you, for instance, come to the conclusion—that I am insane?

Gavin starts

Act I, Scene 2

Doctor (*easily*) No, we didn't.
Carol Or likely to become so?
Gavin Carol, please don't go on like this.
Carol (*ignoring him; still calmly*) Doctor . . . ?
Doctor We came to no—conclusions—about you, Mrs Clevedon; and I've no intention of trying to do so until I've asked you quite a few more questions—(*quickly forestalling Carol, who is about to speak*)—which I *don't* propose to do right now.
Carol Why not?
Doctor (*easily*) "A", because you ought to be resting; and "B"—(*looking at his watch*)—because I have to see another patient in ten minutes' time.
Carol (*after a "duty" smile*) Doctor, do you *believe* that that old woman came to this window?
Doctor (*with firmness*) Now, Mrs Clevedon . . .
Carol (*quietly, but with equal firmness*) Do you? That's all I want to know.
Doctor (*after a slight pause*) *You* are convinced she did, so . . .
Carol (*checking an impatient outburst*) Why can't I be given a straightforward answer to a straightforward question? (*Going on quickly*) Of course *I'm* convinced—but unless *you* are, that doesn't mean a damn thing.
Gavin Carol, don't—don't get excited.
Carol (*to the Doctor; quickly and calmly*) Except, perhaps to convince you that I am—mentally unbalanced.
Doctor (*protesting*) Now, Mrs Clevedon . . .
Carol (*quietly*) Mentally unbalanced—stark raving mad.
Doctor (*gaping at her*) What?
Carol They're the same thing, aren't they?
Doctor (*with a slight show of exasperation*) For heaven's sake . . . ! Of course they're not; not the same thing at all. If you're going to say that everyone who is mentally unbalanced—and aren't we all at times?—everyone who is mentally unbalanced is stark raving mad, then you might as well say a person who takes a couple of aspirin a day is a drug addict.
Carol (*with a smile*) Well, thank you, Doctor, for the comfort you've given me.
Doctor (*warily*) Now what are you . . . ?
Carol (*easily*) It *is* comforting to know I *might* not be raving mad after all, merely—mentally unbalanced.
Doctor I didn't say you are.
Carol You said . . .
Doctor (*keeping his temper with an effort*) Mrs Clevedon, I won't have you twisting my words. I did *not* say you are mentally unbalanced.
Carol (*quietly, easily*) Nor have you assured me that I'm not.
Doctor You don't feel—your normal self at this moment, do you?
Carol Of course I don't.
Doctor Then, you *are*—to a certain extent—mentally unbalanced, but that's nothing to be alarmed about. After the shock you had this morning, it's only natural that you *should* be—temporarily.

Carol The shock I had this morning. You mean seeing that old woman at that window?

Doctor (*firmly*) I mean, your meeting with her in her garden.

Carol (*pointedly*) *And* seeing her at the window.

The Doctor is silent. Carol looks at him intently for quite a while before going on

Do—temporarily unbalanced people imagine they've seen things when they haven't?

Doctor Yes. It is possible.

Carol So I could have *imagined* she came here?

Doctor You could, certainly.

Carol And you're very sure I did, aren't you—(*looking towards Gavin*)—both of you?

Doctor (*coming in quickly before Gavin can reply*) We never said so.

Carol I'd have to be pretty badly—unbalanced—wouldn't I, even allowing for the fright I had this morning—to *imagine* all the horrible details of that old woman standing there at the window with those flowers in her hand—if she hadn't been there at all?

Doctor (*after a slight pause*) When you saw her at the window, was there any—*detail*—about her, *different* from when you saw her this morning?

Carol How do you mean—different?

Doctor Was she, well, *dressed* differently in any way?

Carol She was exactly as she was in the garden.

Doctor H'mm!

Carol (*quickly*) But she *had* the flowers in her hand.

Doctor (*non-committally*) Quite.

Carol And she didn't have them in her hand in the garden.

Doctor I am not going into the ramifications of why it should be so, but there is a reason why you might have imagined the flowers.

Carol (*desperately; under her breath*) Oh, God . . . ! And that's what you think I did, isn't it?

The Doctor is silent

Tell me, when you first saw me seven weeks ago at your surgery—when I first consulted you—did you think I was seriously unbalanced then?

Doctor By no means.

Carol Then why—now?

Doctor Mrs Clevedon, you are under sedation. You should be resting; not torturing your mind like this.

Carol (*moving around restlessly*) There you go again—hedging

Gavin Carol, please, do take the doctor's advice. Go upstairs and . . .

Carol (*flaring up a little*) And what? Throw myself on my bed, curl up, and go fast asleep? You must think me a complete moron if you imagine I could do that. Give me credit for *some*—sensitivity. (*Quickly*) All right! All right! I *will* go up to bed and I shall just lie there—and go *on* torturing myself—wondering if I *am* going round the bend . . .

Doctor Mrs Clevedon . . .

Carol (*turning on him*) Can't you give me the slightest ray of hope? Can't you say to me, "Yes, it is possible the old woman came here"?
Doctor Of course—it's possible.
Carol But you don't think she did, do you?
Doctor (*after a slight pause; quietly*) If I said, "Yes, I do," would you believe me?

Carol looks at him for a long time, then turns and goes quickly out of the room

Gavin moves as if to go after her

(*Quietly*) Let her go.
Gavin Do you think it's safe?
Doctor Safe? Why not? Are you afraid she might be tempted to—to do something—foolish; take an overdose of sleeping pills, f'rinstance?
Gavin You don't think . . . ?
Doctor No, I don't. And I'll tell you why. Don't think I'm speaking unkindly, or unfeelingly about your wife, but—distressed as she undoubtedly is—she is also, in some odd way, enjoying the situation.
Gavin You mean, she isn't actually as—ill—as she appears?
Doctor (*quickly*) Oh, yes, she *is* ill, but in spite of that, she can't help enjoying the—what's the word—the "drama" of this "Lucy" mystery.
Gavin But if the woman didn't come here—then there's no mystery.
Doctor But there is—for your wife, because she is convinced Lucy did come. (*He surreptitiously consults his watch*)
Gavin (*almost to himself*) If only we knew . . . one way or the other.
Doctor You *could* go down to Lucy's place—try to see her—ask her; though I don't give much for your chance of either seeing her, or getting anything out of her.
Gavin Have you ever spoken to her?
Doctor Not really. (*With a wry smile*) Though she's spoken to me.
Gavin She has?
Doctor Given me the rough edge of her tongue—when I was a youngster, that was.
Gavin (*looking hard at the Doctor*) When you . . . ?
Doctor Mind you, I asked for it—the way we used to rag her. (*Looking round*) Now, where did I put my bag?

Gavin looks around, finds the bag and brings it to the Doctor

Gavin Doctor . . .
Doctor Yes?
Gavin I—I . . . (*He breaks away—uncertain*)
Doctor What's on your mind? (*He again takes a quick look at his watch*)
Gavin (*seeing this*) Look, there is something on my mind—something I'd like to discuss with you, but you obviously haven't the time now.
Doctor (*alert*) Something about your wife?
Gavin (*hedging*) Not—directly. About—Dark Lucy. (*Quickly*) I'd rather

not say anything more, just now, but—you did say you were coming in to see Carol tonight?
Doctor Yes.
Gavin Well, could you stay and have a bit of supper and a chat afterwards?
Doctor Yes, I can; it would suit me fine; the wife's out at some meeting or other. I can get round here by about seven? That all right?
Gavin Perfect.
Doctor Good. (*He moves towards the window*) Mind if I go out this way?
Gavin No, of course not.
Doctor (*grinning*) Always like to take a look at other people's gardens; gives me a lot of satisfaction—seeing they're not as good as mine. (*He stoops by the window and picks up a flower near the curtain. He is contemplating the flower as he goes on*) I'm ashamed to confess it, but I get very disgruntled if I find they're better.
Gavin I wish I could work up some enthusiasm about gardening!
Doctor (*still looking at the flower, as a thought strikes him*) Good God!
Gavin What . . . ?

The Doctor is staring at the flower

What have you got there?
Doctor (*quietly*) There are none of these in *your* garden, are there?
Gavin (*vaguely*) What . . . ? (*Looking at the flower*) I don't think so. I don't remember ever seeing . . .
Doctor I'm damned sure there aren't. Your predecessor was no gardener, and these take a lot of looking after to get 'em to bloom.
Gavin What flower is it?
Doctor Gentian. I've never had any luck with 'em. (*Suddenly*) I'm going up to see your wife. (*He crosses towards the door*)
Gavin But . . .
Doctor (*quietly*) To tell her she can stop worrying herself silly, and to apologize for doubting her. (*Turning to Gavin*) And when I come down, it wouldn't be a bad idea if you went up and did the same.
Gavin (*mystified*) But . . .
Doctor (*overlapping*) I know of only one garden in this village where these things are grown. I don't have to tell you whose it is, do I?
Gavin (*as he realizes the implication*) Flowers in her hand . . . ! Then that means she *did* . . .
Doctor (*opening the door*) That's *just* what it means. (*Turning and speaking quietly and significantly*) And just *what* does *that* mean?

The Doctor holds Gavin's gaze for a moment, then goes out, closing the door behind him

Gavin turns slowly and stands looking towards the window, as—

the CURTAIN *falls*

ACT II

The same. A quarter past seven, the same evening

When the CURTAIN *rises, Gavin and the Doctor are discovered in the room. The curtains are not drawn, but the lights are on. The Doctor is seated in an armchair. An empty sherry glass is beside him. He is lost in troubled thought. Gavin, watching him, goes to the empty glass, picks it up, refills it, then returns it to the table by the Doctor*

Doctor (*with a little start, realizing the glass has been refilled*) Oh! Thanks! I didn't intend to have another, but . . .

Gavin You look as if you could do with it. I'm afraid I've—shaken you a bit, haven't I?

Doctor I'll say you have! More than a bit; a whole lot. It's—it's fantastic, that is if it's true, and dammit it must be—must be.

Gavin What do you know about her—Lucy?

Doctor Practically nothing. She lives in the village—a distinctive part of it, you might say—but she keeps herself very much to herself—always has.

Gavin Do you know when she first came to live here—or was she . . . ? (*Quickly*) What's her surname by the way? Grace doesn't even know that.

Doctor (*thinking hard*) Oh Lord! What the devil is it? It must be a lifetime since I heard it. Er, Man—Man—Man—something. Manningham? No! Man—er, *Manning*, that's it.

Gavin Manning. And do you know, was she born in the village or . . .

Doctor No, she wasn't born here; came when I was a child, a baby, really.

Gavin You've never attended her professionally?

Doctor No, nor did my father. Goodness knows whether she ever *is* ill. If so I suppose she doses herself with herbs and what not—she looks the type.

Gavin (*moving around*) H'm! But can you accept that she must be—at least—a hundred and ten years old?

Doctor God! It's a disturbing thought, isn't it, that she *might* be that age? Have you spoken about this to anyone else—except Grace?

Gavin No.

Doctor Not to your wife?

Gavin No

Doctor I shouldn't, if I were you. The sooner she gets old Lucy out of her mind, the better now. She's far less—strained—this evening, I'm glad to see.

Gavin I haven't known her so—relaxed for weeks. It's quite remarkable.

Doctor H'm! I don't want to be a Job's comforter, but don't count on it lasting. It can only be temporary—as yet. It's just that she's so—relieved, to know that she *did* see Lucy at that window.

Gavin (*moving around restlessly*) Lucy . . .

Doctor (*troubled*) Yes—Lucy. (*Suddenly*) Why the devil are we worrying our heads about her? What does it matter if she *is* a hundred and ten—*five* hundred and ten?

Gavin Us—you and I—knowing, that wouldn't matter I suppose. But how long is it going to be before someone else in the village realizes it?

Doctor It's incredible that it never occurred to *me*; that you, a newcomer to the village, had to point it out.

Gavin (*moving to the window*) Perhaps so, and yet, in a way it's understandable that having known her all your life you should accept her as part and parcel of the village. Just as the Parish Council have accepted the War Memorial out there for years without, consciously, realizing that it was falling into a state of disrepair. They were genuinely staggered when I pointed the fact out to them.

Doctor (*muttering*) Yes, I see your point.

Gavin By the way, the cottage—is it Lucy's own property?

Doctor It is; otherwise it wouldn't've been allowed to get in the state it's in.

Gavin You've never been inside yourself?

Doctor Nobody has, to my knowledge. (*With a grin*) Mind you, I've never pressed for an invitation.

Gavin It must be appalling—if the outside is anything to go by.

Doctor *And* its owner!

Carol enters through the door. She wears a cocktail dress

Gavin (*seeing her*) Oh!

Carol (*quite amiably*) Five minutes?

Gavin (*puzzled*) H'm?

Carol Supper in five minutes?

Gavin Oh! Yes! Yes!

Carol I hope you won't mind, Doctor, but it's cold.

Doctor Not at all.

Carol Scotch salmon and salad.

Doctor (*delighted*) *Scotch* salmon!

Carol (*smiling*) The real McCoy. I wouldn't dare offer you anything but.

Doctor (*ruefully*) I *am* in the wrong profession! Scotch salmon! Am I drooling?

Carol Five minutes then. (*She is about to go out, then hesitates as if about to speak*)

Gavin (*noticing this*) Yes, dear?

Carol (*with a smile*) It'll keep.

Carol exits

Gavin and the Doctor both, almost unconsciously stand looking towards the

Act II

door after Carol's exit. Then they—again almost unconsciously—look towards each other, then, somewhat guiltily, pull themselves together

Doctor (*quietly*) Carol—you don't mind if I call her Carol?
Gavin Of course not.
Doctor She does seem on top of the world tonight?
Gavin (*quietly*) Yes. (*After a slight pause*) Was that—all—you were going to say?

The Doctor looks at Gavin quizzically

You're—puzzled—aren't you, as to why Lucy came here this morning?
Doctor Everything about Lucy puzzles me—now.
Gavin Now that you know how old she must be.
Doctor (*moving restlessly*) I've got to accept it—her age. I've got to, although my every instinct, as a medical man, tells me it can't be so. But I've got to believe that a woman, well over a hundred years old came to that window—to see your wife.
Gavin But we know there was no physical effort involved . . .
Doctor I'm not thinking of the physical side of it. The frightening thing to me is that her brain hasn't deteriorated any more than her physique. Damn it, at her age, there should be no brain left at all. Yet her coming here wasn't just aimless wandering; it was deliberate, I'm sure of that. But why? Why?
Gavin Couldn't it be that she wanted to apologize to Carol for frightening her?
Doctor (*not too convincingly*) It could be.
Gavin But you don't think it was?
Doctor (*shaking his head almost wildly*) I don't know. I don't know! The whole business—there's something—uncanny about it.
Gavin Un . . . ?
Doctor Damned uncanny!
Gavin But . . .

The front-door bell rings. They both give an uncomfortable little start

Doctor (*with a little laugh*) Good Lord! Don't say she's come to the *front door* now!
Gavin (*moving to the door*) I hardly think so. (*He opens it, looking out*) Oh! Carol's there already. (*He closes the door again*) I hope it isn't someone wanting to *see* me.
Doctor So do I. I'm hungry.
Gavin Another drink?
Doctor No, thanks.

Carol comes in, closing the door after her

Carol It's a parishioner—a Mrs Wilson . . .
Doctor (*in mock dismay*) Oh Lord! Mrs "Matter of Fact" Wilson!
Carol (*puzzled*) Mrs . . . ?
Doctor (*coughing embarrassedly*) Sorry, I shouldn't have . . . (*Grinning*)

Er, my nickname for her. (*In a despairing voice*) Not wanting me, surely? I saw her only a couple of days ago.
Carol No. She wants to see you, Gavin. I told her we were just going to have a meal and that we had a guest but—(*after a shrug of the shoulders*)—she seems rather upset about something.
Gavin Then I must see her. After all, she is one of my faithful very few. D'you mind?
Doctor (*grinning*) You don't care a damn whether I mind or not. Have her in. I'll just have a word with her, then join you in the kitchen if I may, Mrs Clevedon?
Carol Do, please. Thank goodness it's a cold meal.

Carol exits, partly closing the door

Doctor (*in an undertone, with one eye on the door*) Hope you've learned the trick of cutting 'em short?
Gavin Cutting 'em . . . ?
Doctor Mrs Wilson's one of those women who'll keep you all night if you *don't* shut her up. I'm a past master at that game.
Gavin You must give me a few lessons.

There is a knock at the door

(*Heartily*) Come in, Mrs Wilson!

The door opens and Mrs Wilson appears. She is a woman of around forty-seven to fifty, quietly dressed, inoffensive, and shows a certain nervousness in conversation

Good evening. Come and sit down.
Mrs Wilson Good evening, Vicar. I'm sorry to . . . (*She sees the Doctor*) Oh! Good evening, Doctor. (*She stands in the doorway*)
Doctor 'Evening.
Mrs Wilson I didn't know you were . . .
Doctor (*cutting in*) Not to worry. I'll leave you with the Vicar.
Mrs Wilson (*quickly*) Oh, but . . .
Doctor (*cutting in*) Just wanted to know how you were.
Mrs Wilson Well, as a matter of fact I'm . . .
Doctor (*cutting in*) Arthritis easier?
Mrs Wilson Well, as a matter of . . .
Doctor (*cutting in*) Get those tablets I prescribed?
Mrs Wilson Well, yes. I went over to . . .
Doctor (*cutting in*) Taking 'em regularly?
Mrs Wilson Well as a matter of fact, I . . .
Doctor No use if you don't, you know. Well now, I'll leave you to have your chat with the Vicar.

The Doctor moves towards the door. Mrs Wilson is still in the doorway

Mrs Wilson Well, as a matter of fact, I . . .

Act II

Doctor (*waggishly*) Two's company, eh?
Mrs Wilson (*in a burst to get it in*) I'd be glad if you'd stay, Doctor.
Doctor (*pulling up*) Eh?
Mrs Wilson You might be able to help.
Doctor Oh, but . . .
Mrs Wilson As a matter of fact I nearly came to you instead of the Vicar. After all I've known you longer, haven't I?
Doctor Yes, but . . .
Gavin Would you *rather* speak to the Doctor, Mrs Wilson? (*Moving as if to go*) If so . . .
Mrs Wilson (*flustered*) Oh, no, sir. You can stay.
Gavin (*with a wry smile*) Thank you.
Mrs Wilson After all, they do say two heads are better than one, don't they?
Gavin They do indeed. Well, come and sit down.

Mrs Wilson sits on an upright chair near the desk

Doctor (*to Gavin, picking up his glass*) May I change my mind?
Gavin Do! Er, can I offer *you* a sherry, Mrs Wilson, or . . . ?

The Doctor goes to pour himself a drink

Mrs Wilson No, thank you, Vicar. As a matter of fact, I'm not partial to intoxicating liquor.
Gavin (*guiltily*) Oh! Oh well . . .
Mrs Wilson You see, I saw what it did to my husband.
Gavin Oh!
Mrs Wilson You saw, too, didn't you, Doctor?

The Doctor, about to pour himself a sherry, stops, and puts down the decanter and glass

Doctor (*dejectedly*) Yes. Yes.
Mrs Wilson It was the death of him, wasn't it, Doctor? (*Turning to Gavin*) That's between these four walls, Vicar.
Gavin Er—quite!

Gavin looks somewhat helplessly towards the Doctor who is behind Mrs Wilson. The Doctor—to Gavin's embarrassment—gives him an enormous wink, then pours himself a sherry. Mrs Wilson, not seeing this, is searching in her bag for a handkerchief

(*To Mrs Wilson, embarrassed*) Well—er—now! What . . . ? (*He sits at his desk*)
Mrs Wilson I'm worried, Vicar.
Gavin Oh, I'm sorry. If I—we—can . . .
Mrs Wilson (*producing her handkerchief*) As a matter of fact I'm at my wits' end!
Gavin (*murmuring sympathetically*) Oh dear!
Mrs Wilson Otherwise I wouldn't've troubled you, especially when Mrs

Clevedon told me you were just going to have a meal, and that you had a guest.
Gavin Don't worry about that.
Mrs Wilson (*innocently*) No, I won't—seeing that it's only the doctor.

The Doctor, by the drinks table, is just taking a surreptitious sip at his sherry. He obviously chokes, but does so silently

Gavin (*aware of the Doctor's choke*) Er, what is troubling you, Mrs Wilson?
Mrs Wilson It's my daughter, sir.
Gavin Oh!
Mrs Wilson Doris. (*With a big sigh*) That girl's been a millstone round my neck since the day she left school.

Gavin murmurs sympathetically

You know that, don't you, Doctor? (*She turns to the Doctor*)

The Doctor, as Mrs Wilson begins to turn, surreptitiously puts the glass behind his back

Doctor Eh? Oh yes, yes.
Gavin But what has she—er . . . ?
Mrs Wilson She's—she's disappeared, sir.
Gavin *What?*

The Doctor does not show Gavin's shock

Mrs Wilson Hasn't been home for two days and nights.
Gavin But—you mean you've heard nothing from her, or of her, for two days?
Mrs Wilson No, sir. And it's driving me out of my mind. A young girl like her . . .
Gavin How old is she? I'm afraid I've never met her.
Mrs Wilson She's only eighteen. (*She dabs her eyes*)
Gavin Eighteen. Has she any relations she would be likely to go to?
Mrs Wilson She's only an auntie in Scotland, and Doris hates the sight of her.
Gavin Does she go out to work?
Mrs Wilson Doris? She's behind the jewellery counter in Woolworth's at Badcaster. She goes over by bus every day.
Gavin And she hasn't been at work these last two days?
Mrs Wilson No, sir. And they're wanting to know what's what, and I don't know what to tell 'em.
Gavin But—when did you see her last?
Mrs Wilson When she went gaddin' out on Tuesday night, after she'd had her meal.
Gavin Tuesday! But today's Friday! That means she hasn't been home for *three* nights!
Mrs Wilson No, sir.
Gavin Have you been in touch with the police?

Act II

Mrs Wilson No, sir, and as a matter of fact, that's what I wanted your advice about. D'you think I ought to do that—go to the police, I mean?
Gavin But of course you must, Mrs Wilson. You should have done it before this.
Mrs Wilson But I've been hoping every minute that she'd turn up and if she had've done, and if I had been on to the police she'd've . . . Well, you've no idea what a temper she has when she's roused.
Gavin (*firmly*) Mrs Wilson, this ought to be reported to the police at once.
Mrs Wilson If you say so, sir. (*Hesitantly*) But . . .
Gavin But what?
Mrs Wilson (*uneasily*) I don't *want* to report it, not if I can help it, but—(*resignedly*)—if you think it best . . . ?
Gavin I most certainly do.
Mrs Wilson (*after hesitation*) Very well, sir.
Gavin I'll get on the phone right away. You feel—able to speak to them?
Mrs Wilson Could *you* do it, sir? I get flustered on the phone, and . . .
Gavin Yes, of course, but we'd better get all the facts down on paper before we . . . (*He draws a pad and pencil to him*) Now, where do we begin? Doris's age—eighteen, you said?
Mrs Wilson Yes, sir.
Gavin Is she dark or fair?
Mrs Wilson Well, as a matter of fact her hair's dark brown like mine used to be, but she's had it done blonde like so many of these youngsters nowadays. I told her I thought it looked awful, but . . .
Gavin Er, what was she wearing the last time you saw her?
Mrs Wilson Wearing? Well now, let me think. I remember she had her new green coat on, 'cos . . .
Gavin Er, what height would you say?

The Doctor has been a silent onlooker during the foregoing. He now moves down into the scene

Doctor (*after a little cough*) Er, if I may interrupt . . . ?
Mrs Wilson (*turning to him*) Oh yes, please, Doctor, do. I'd be ever so grateful.
Gavin (*apologetically to the Doctor*) I'm so sorry. I'd almost forgotten . . .
Doctor (*after a "not to worry" wave of the hand; to Mrs Wilson*) Mrs Wilson . . .
Mrs Wilson Yes, Doctor?
Doctor Before the Vicar gets on to the police, I think there's something he ought to know—and which *you* ought to bear in mind.
Gavin Oh?
Doctor (*to Mrs Wilson, gently and quietly*) Doris. This isn't the *first* time she's—disappeared?
Mrs Wilson (*after a little start*) I—I . . .

Gavin looks up in surprise

Doctor It isn't, is it?
Mrs Wilson (*almost in a whisper*) No, Doctor.

Doctor (*gently*) About six months ago, she went off for a few nights, didn't she?
Mrs Wilson (*almost inaudibly*) Yes.
Doctor (*as before*) With—a man.

Mrs Wilson cries silently into her handkerchief for a while. The Doctor and Gavin exchange looks. Gavin automatically pushes the pad away from him a little

Mrs Wilson (*at last*) I—I didn't think anyone knew. I thought we'd managed to hush it up.
Doctor It isn't easy to hush such things up; not in a small village like this.
Mrs Wilson D'you mean—*everyone* knows?

The Doctor shrugs his shoulders

Gavin (*gently*) Do you know the man? Could she have gone with him again?
Mrs Wilson No, I don't know who he was. Doris'd never let on. But she couldn't've gone far away with him—not that time.
Doctor Why not?
Mrs Wilson 'Cos she still went to work every day. She—she just didn't come home at nights.
Doctor But this time . . . ?
Mrs Wilson She hasn't been near her work. She's just—disappeared.
Gavin (*rather helplessly, appealing to the Doctor*) Well, what do we . . . ?
Doctor The sensible thing is, of course, to ring the police, but I think Mrs Wilson here, should fully understand that once we do that, and when the police find Doris . . .
Mrs Wilson (*anxiously*) They wouldn't take her away from me, would they?
Doctor No, they wouldn't do that—at eighteen she's *supposed* to be old enough to know what she's doing—and it's a pity because—and I don't want to sound callous, Mrs Wilson—but a couple of years in a remand home would probably do Doris all the good in the world.
Mrs Wilson (*sobbing into her handkerchief*) Oh, don't say that, Doctor My only child . . . (*She continues to cry—not noisily—into her handkerchief*)

Carol knocks on the door and immediately enters

Carol (*as she enters*) I'm sorry to interrupt, but . . . (*She is at once aware of Mrs Wilson's distress*) Oh, I'm sorry! What . . . ? Can I . . . ? (*She involuntarily moves towards Mrs Wilson*)
Gavin No, no. It's—I'm sorry, Carol, but we'll have to delay supper for a while yet.

Carol is very near Mrs Wilson, who, becoming aware of her presence and nearness, turns to her in her own almost abandoned distress and puts her arms out to her

Act II

Mrs Wilson (*brokenly*) Oh—Mrs Cleveland ...

Carol instinctively, and in genuine compassion, puts her arms around Mrs Wilson

Carol (*quietly*) Oh, you poor soul! (*To the others*) What ... ?
Gavin (*hesitantly*) Mrs Wilson is—naturally—very upset, I can't tell you why, Carol, but ...
Mrs Wilson (*brokenly*) Tell her, sir; tell Mrs Clevedon. What's it matter? Everybody'll know sooner or later.
Gavin (*after a slight pause*) Mrs Wilson's eighteen-year-old daughter hasn't been home for three nights. There's every likelihood that she's gone off with a man.
Carol (*under her breath*) Oh, no!
Gavin We're trying to decide whether to contact the police or not.
Carol (*practically*) Shall I stay? Mrs Wilson, would you like me to?
Mrs Wilson Oh, please. I'd be so grateful. Though you must be wanting to get on with your meal.
Carol Never mind about that. It's a cold meal, anyway. Come and sit over here with me. (*She takes Mrs Wilson across to the settee, sits her down then sits by her, taking one of her hands in her own*)

Gavin is obviously surprised at the complete change in Carol. He looks towards the Doctor, who gives him a reassuring smile

(*To Gavin and the Doctor, not aggressively*) Why are you hesitating about contacting the police? I should have thought it was the obvious thing to do.
Mrs Wilson If that's what she *has* done—gone off with a man, I can't bear the thought of the scandal there'd be—not again.
Carol Again?
Doctor This isn't the first time Doris has done this.
Carol Oh, I see.

Mrs Wilson again weeps silently into her handkerchief. Carol comforts her silently before speaking

Did the police bring Doris back the last time?
Mrs Wilson No, she was only away two nights; came back on her own.
Doctor But everyone in the village knew about it.

There is silence for a moment, save for Mrs Wilson's occasional sob into her handkerchief

Carol (*speaking generally*) You don't know for certain that she has gone off with some man?
Doctor It's the obvious explanation I would say.
Carol (*not very convincingly*) Of course she could've—— (*She hesitates*)
Gavin Could what?
Carol (*after a look towards Mrs Wilson; quietly*)—have had an accident.
Doctor She's been away three nights. Something would have been heard of it.

Carol Did she have any—much money with her?
Mrs Wilson Money?
Carol When she left home, I mean.
Mrs Wilson That's another thing that's worried me about her lately.
Carol What is?
Mrs Wilson This last few months—the money Doris 'as had, and spent—far more than she's ever earned at her job. The clothes she's bought—expensive too. Goodness knows what she paid for her new green coat—the one she went off in. And the Lord knows how much it costs her to have her hair blonded up every so often.
Carol I suppose the man . . . (*She breaks off*) You have no idea where Doris might've gone—or who the man might be?
Mrs Wilson No. I haven't. But it'll be someone she's met in Badcaster, not here in the village.
Carol Would any of her friends know?
Mrs Wilson Friends?
Carol Well, she must have friends—girl friends of her own age in the village, surely?
Mrs Wilson Doris has never had much to do with the girls in the village. Always thought herself a cut above them, though goodness knows why; she'd no cause to.
Carol (*to Gavin*) She doesn't belong to your Youth Club, or anything like that?
Gavin No. I've never even met her.
Carol But when she comes home from work—after she's had her meal—what does she do?
Mrs Wilson Goes straight out again most nights.
Carol Where?
Mrs Wilson (*after a slight pause*) She never says.
Carol You mean, you don't ask her where she's going, or, when she comes back, where she's been?
Mrs Wilson (*with a little sob*) I've given up asking her. It's wrong of me, I suppose; but—when I did used to ask her it was like trying to get blood out of a stone.
Carol (*after a pause*) But she *must* be friendly with *someone* in the village. Can't you think of anyone?
Mrs Wilson (*as a thought occurs to her*) Oh!
Carol Yes?
Mrs Wilson (*after a pause*) I don't know about "friendly". But, as a matter of fact, there is—(*she looks round as if scared*)—there is *someone* she goes to see—or used to. I don't know if she still does.
Doctor Who's that?
Mrs Wilson (*quietly*) I don't like to say.
Doctor (*again irritably*) For heaven's sake . . .
Mrs Wilson (*not listening*) 'Sides, you might not believe me.
Doctor (*with control*) Now, Mrs Wilson, you say you don't want to go to the police, but you want to know where Doris is, naturally; so if you know of something—or someone who might have an idea . . .

Act II

Mrs Wilson But you'll say it doesn't make sense—that *she* wouldn't have —she couldn't.
Doctor Who wouldn't what? Come on, let's have it.
Mrs Wilson (*reluctantly*) Well, you'll hardly believe this, Doctor; I can hardly believe it myself. I was struck dumb when I first heard about it.
Doctor (*wearily*) About what?
Mrs Wilson As a matter of fact it was Mrs Bradley, four doors along from me, who told me in the first place.

The Doctor, Gavin and Carol all instinctively open their mouths as if to ask "Told you what?" and all decide against it. They smile at each other quietly. Mrs Wilson has been unaware of the foregoing

She swore her husband used to see Doris going there; actually going through the door.
Doctor (*almost irritably under his breath, as he moves away*) For Go— Pete's sake!
Carol (*hurriedly, with eye on the Doctor*) Going where, Mrs Wilson?
Mrs Wilson (*to Carol*) I don't suppose you'll know who I mean, not having been here for long, but—(*to the Doctor*)—you will, Doctor. Joe Bradley swears he's seen Doris going into—into Dark Lucy's place.

The others stiffen. Carol gives an audible gasp. There is a stunned silence for a moment. The Doctor and Gavin unconsciously look towards Carol

Gavin (*anxiously*) Carol, hadn't you better leave *us* to . . .
Carol (*with the old strained look on her face; sharply*) No!
Gavin But, darling . . .
Carol (*almost snapping*) I'm staying!
Gavin But . . . (*He looks helplessly towards the Doctor*)
Carol (*seeing this*) No matter what the Doctor says, I'm staying.

The Doctor shrugs his shoulders. Mrs Wilson is becoming aware of an "atmosphere"

Mrs Wilson (*bewildered*) What . . . ? Is there something . . . ?
Carol (*with her eyes defiantly on the men, but patting Mrs Wilson's hand*) It's all right, Mrs Wilson.
Doctor Mrs Wilson, were you serious when you said what you did just now?
Mrs Wilson (*flustered*) You mean . . . ?
Doctor I mean about Doris going to old Lucy's cottage.
Mrs Wilson Joe Bradley swears to it, his wife says. And you know Joe, Doctor. He's not the sort to say things just for the sake of creating trouble, is he?
Doctor (*quietly*) No.
Mrs Wilson As a matter of fact, he saw her a few times and always she— sort of—sneaked in, as if she didn't want to be seen, like. Joe has an allotment down River Lane, nearly opposite Dark Lucy's place. That's how he . . .
Doctor (*stunned*) It's incredible! I can't believe . . .

Mrs Wilson That's what I said when I . . .
Doctor I've never heard of Lucy letting *anyone* into her cottage.
Gavin (*to the Doctor*) I suppose Bradley *is*—reliable?
Doctor (*almost impatiently*) Good God, yes. *And* there's nothing wrong with his eyesight.
Carol (*to Mrs Wilson*) Did you speak to your daughter about this?
Mrs Wilson Yes, I did. As soon as I heard about it, I spoke to her that very night.
Carol And what did she say?
Mrs Wilson (*after a slight pause*) She denied it.
Carol She . . . ?
Mrs Wilson But she was lying to me—I could tell.
Carol Did she persist in—lying?
Mrs Wilson She did for ever so long, but I kept on at her, and in the end she admitted that she had been there.
Carol But she doesn't go now?
Mrs Wilson I don't think so, but Joe Bradley's been laid up this last couple of months, so . . .
Doctor Did Doris say *why* she went there?
Mrs Wilson (*after a slight pause*) She said she had a right to go where she liked, and if she wanted to help the old woman what business was it of anybody elses. That's what she *said*.
Doctor *Help* her? Help *Lucy?* But that's damned nonsense. She's never let anybody help her.
Mrs Wilson 'Course she hasn't, and if it was housework Doris was trying to make me believe she was helping with, well I just *won't* believe it. I've never known Doris do a hand's turn at home, without being badgered into it.
Carol Then why do you think she *did* go?
Mrs Wilson I don't know! I just don't know—and it frightens me to think of it. One thing I'm certain of—she didn't go of her own free will!
Carol (*gaping at her*) Didn't . . . ?
Mrs Wilson (*getting agitated*) Does it stand to reason that she would? I mean, what can a young girl like Doris have in common with Dark Lucy?
Carol But if she didn't go of her own free will, then . . . (*After a slight pause*) What are you suggesting?
Mrs Wilson (*almost terrified to say it*) *She* forced her to go!
Doctor Now, Mrs Wilson, that's . . .
Mrs Wilson (*wildly*) She did, Doctor, she did. Don't ask me how; it's all part of her wicked witchcraft.
Carol (*almost shouting*) What?
Mrs Wilson I don't care what anyone says—she's a witch!
Carol Witch!

The Doctor looks quickly towards Gavin. Gavin is puzzled by the look

Mrs Wilson (*in an awed voice*) She is, I *know* she is.
Carol You *know* . . . ?

Act II

Gavin (*trying to speak lightly*) Now, Mrs Wilson, you really shouldn't . . .
Carol (*gripping Mrs Wilson's arm*) How—how do you *know*?
Gavin (*urgently*) Carol, will you please . . .
Carol (*insistently*) How do you know?
Gavin (*firmly*) Carol!
Carol (*suddenly blazing out at Gavin*) Shut up, damn you!
Gavin (*stung; loudly*) Carol!
Carol (*ignoring him; to Mrs Wilson, intensely*) Mrs Wilson, listen to me—please, listen to me. I *have* seen that old woman. I saw her this morning.
Gavin (*almost at the same time; to the Doctor, desperately*) Doctor, can't you speak to Carol; make her . . .
Carol (*overlapping this*) She tried to—get hold of me.
Mrs Wilson Oh, no!
Doctor (*overlapping*) Mrs Clevedon, you're doing yourself no good getting worked up like this.
Carol (*overlapping*) She put her arms round me . . .

Mrs Wilson gives a cry of horror and disgust

I knew she was loathsome—evil . . .
Mrs Wilson (*almost wildly*) She is! That's just what she is.
Carol (*not heeding; almost racing on*) I sensed it. I've been racking my brain to think what it *was* about her that was so—repellent. It wasn't just that she was—foul—dirty. I knew there was something else—something—unnatural . . .
Gavin (*almost shouting*) Mrs Wilson, don't listen to all this nonsense.
Mrs Wilson (*desperately and fervently*) It isn't nonsense, sir. Believe me it isn't. I *know! I* know she's a witch! I have proof!

Carol is by now in a tremendous state of excitement

Carol (*to the others*) You hear? You *hear*? (*To Mrs Wilson*) What proof have you, Mrs Wilson?
Gavin (*advancing slightly on Carol*) Carol, for you own good, will you leave us, or must I . . . ?

Carol rises and springs back a little, facing Gavin, with hands slightly outstretched, fingers wide apart

Carol (*very intensely*) You come near me, and I'll . . .
Doctor (*almost shouting*) Mrs Clevedon!
Mrs Wilson (*at the same time; brokenly*) Oh . . . no!

There is a dead pause. Gavin can only stare at Carol for quite a while, incapable of speech. The tremendous hurt shows in his eyes. Slowly, Carol's hands go down to her side. Then Gavin turns and moves slowly to the desk, where he stands half turned away from the others. Once, he brushes a hand across his eyes. Carol sees this gesture and is at once contrite. She goes to Gavin.

Carol Oh, my darling—Gavin—(*brokenly*)—I didn't mean—I—I—please tell me you forgive me. I shouldn't have said . . .

As Gavin does not turn to her, she puts her hands on his shoulders, and her face against his back

> But, darling, can't you *understand*? I've got to know the truth about that old woman. I've got to, Gavin! If I don't, I—I—I'm so terrified I'll go out of my mind. I know I'm not well. If I were, perhaps what happened this morning—it wouldn't have had the effect on me that it has. I know you and the Doctor think you're acting for the best when you tell me I must stop thinking about the old woman, but—in the condition I'm in—I can't. If I leave you to talk to Mrs Wilson, God knows what ideas I'll get into my head. Please let me stay—let me hear what Mrs Wilson can tell us. Gavin, please!

Doctor But, Mrs Clevedon, we're trying to solve the mystery of Doris's disappearance—there's no suggestion that Lucy has any connection with that.
Carol How do you know?
Mrs Wilson (*to whom this is a fresh thought*) What? Oh, don't say that!
Carol I'm not saying it is so . . .
Gavin I should hope not.
Carol But you can't dismiss the possibility. If the old woman *is* a witch . . .

Gavin moves, exasperated

> If she *is* a witch—who knows?—she may be holding the girl, somehow, against her will.

Gavin Carol!
Carol All right! All right! But if she *isn't* a witch—just a friend of Doris—she may know *where* she is—*who* she's with. Doris may have told her.
Gavin (*contemptuously*) A witch! I've never heard such . . .
Carol You've heard what Mrs Wilson has said. She's told us she has proof that she *is*. Don't you think you ought to hear that proof before you begin scoffing?

Gavin looks towards the Doctor, who gives an almost helpless shrug of the shoulders

Gavin (*to Mrs Wilson, in a flat voice*) Mrs Wilson, what *is* this proof?

Carol again sits by Mrs Wilson on the settee. Gavin moves to the desk and stands half turned away from the others as he listens

Doctor (*meanwhile*) And why have you kept quiet about it till now?
Mrs Wilson (*obviously uneasy in her mind*) I had my reasons then.
Doctor What . . . ?
Mrs Wilson (*after a slight pause*) I was scared of what *she* might do to me.
Doctor *Lucy*, do to *you*?
Mrs Wilson (*in a whisper*) Yes.
Doctor What *could* she do to you? You never go near her, do you? (*Before Mrs Wilson can reply; almost gaping at her*) You don't mean—what she might do to you—by *witchcraft*?
Mrs Wilson (*still in a whisper*) Yes, that's just what I do mean. Same as she did to—to my mother.

Act II

Doctor (*with a start*) Your mother? But . . .
Mrs Wilson You remember, her, don't you, Doctor?
Doctor (*uneasily*) Yes, yes, of course. But, Mrs Wilson, do you think you ought to . . .
Mrs Wilson (*overlapping*) And you know how she died, don't you?
Doctor (*uneasily*) Yes, yes, but . . .
Mrs Wilson How everybody—the Coroner—everybody, *said* she died.
Doctor (*placatingly*) Now why . . . ?
Mrs Wilson Accident—that's what everybody said—but it wasn't! *I know* it wasn't.

The Doctor, with a shrug of resignation, moves away. Gavin faces Mrs Wilson, who speaks to Carol

(*After a slight pause; falteringly*) It must've been . . . thirty years since it —happened. Mother always liked to go for a bit of a walk after she'd had her tea, and sometimes, I used to go with her. One night we happened to go down River Lane, and as we were passing Dark Lucy's place, Mother made a remark about the filthy windows and curtains, and she said it was high time somebody did something about Lucy— had her turned out of her cottage—put in a home. (*After a slight pause*) She hadn't seen Lucy in the garden, but she must've heard what Mother said, 'cos the next thing, she was through the gate shouting and screaming something dreadful. She grabbed Mother by one of her shoulders and—she spat in her face, and she made some sort of—sign with her hand, then she ran back into the garden—laughing—and laughing. I can still hear her laughing whenever I think about it. It wasn't a human laugh, I swear it wasn't.
Carol (*scarcely audible*) Oh—God!
Mrs Wilson How I got Mother home I'll never know. And—(*after a slight pause*)—from that very night, she began to fail. Within a matter of a few days, she changed from a fine healthy woman to a—a nervous wreck. She wouldn't let us send for you, Doctor. She never went out, not shopping or anything, till—(*she pauses*)—one evening I—I bullied her to come out with me for a bit. (*She pauses*) We were passing the post office, not a soul in sight, nothing except a motor lorry that was coming along towards us. (*She pauses*) And then it happened.
Carol (*at last; gently*) What happened, Mrs Wilson?
Mrs Wilson (*controlling herself*) All of a sudden—just as the lorry was getting near us, Mother sort of stumbled, and—she just fell into the road—in front of the lorry.
Carol (*scarcely audible*) How—dreadful!
Mrs Wilson (*to the Doctor, quietly*) You remember, don't you, Doctor?
Doctor (*quietly*) I remember. (*To the others, quietly*) Someone phoned me. I got there in a matter of minutes, but of course there was nothing I could do.
Mrs Wilson But you don't know what happened while we were waiting for you, Doctor—and nobody else does; nobody noticed—except me.
Doctor (*quietly*) What did happen?

Mrs Wilson Something made me look up and—there was Dark Lucy on the pavement, just walking past, and I could see she was—was grinning to herself. She was, I swear it! She never so much as turned her head to look and see what had happened. (*Slightly hysterically*) She didn't *have* to look 'cos she *knew*—she *knew*—(*breaking down completely*) —'cos with her wicked witchcraft she'd made it happen! And nothing anyone can say'll make me think otherwise.
Doctor (*quietly*) Thank goodness you said nothing of this at the inquest.
Mrs Wilson (*after a slight pause*) There was only one reason why I kept quiet. 'Cos I was a coward, that's why. I was—scared—of what that old woman might *do* if I did tell the truth. I was scared that she'd make something like what happened to Mother happen to *me*. That's why I daren't breathe a word about it.
Doctor Why have you told *us* now?

Mrs Wilson looks at him questioningly

(*Quietly*) Lucy is still alive. If you think she's a witch, aren't you—scared—she might still do you a mischief?

There is an embarrassed pause

Gavin (*at last*) Look! Aren't we straying somewhat from our chief concern? Surely it's Doris's disappearance we must concentrate on. I can't see any connection between that and—(*to Mrs Wilson*)—your mother's death, Mrs Wilson.

Carol looks at Gavin almost pityingly

(*Aware of the look and turning, somewhat stung, to Carol*) Well, can *you*?

Carol slowly looks away, but says nothing

(*To Mrs Wilson*) You don't seriously think, do you, Mrs Wilson, that Lucy has anything to do with *that*—Doris's disappearance?

Mrs Wilson looks at Gavin helplessly

(*Desperately*) It's—it's too absurd.
Carol (*sharply*) Why is it? Is it any more absurd than the fact that Doris goes to Dark Lucy's place? Or don't you believe that either?

Gavin is silent

And why *does* she go there? An eighteen-year-old girl? She can't go there because she *wants* to—I'll never believe that. (*To the Doctor*) Do you, Doctor?
Doctor (*troubled*) It takes a bit of believing. Doris isn't—(*to Mrs Wilson*)—and you've said this yourself, Mrs Wilson, so I'm not treading on any corns—Doris isn't exactly the ministering angel type.
Carol Then *why does* she go there?
Doctor (*after a pause; with a troubled sigh*) I dunno. I can't think of any reason.

Carol You mean you won't let yourself accept the only possible reason—the one Mrs Wilson has already given us—that Dark Lucy *forces* her to go?

Doctor I'm sorry, but that's just damned ridiculous. How could an old woman a hundred and God knows how many years old, possibly . . .

Carol (*cutting in; completely staggered*) What? (*After a slight pause; pointedly*) How old did you say she is?

Doctor (*after cursing himself under his breath*) Now, look, Mrs Clevedon . . . (*He tails off miserably*)

Carol rises and stares at Gavin, then the Doctor. They both look very uneasy

Carol (*in an awestricken voice*) Is that true—that that old woman is over a hundred years old?

Doctor (*growling*) Yes, it is.

Carol (*turning to Mrs Wilson*) Did you know that, Mrs Wilson?

Mrs Wilson Well, as a matter of fact, I've never thought about it, not properly. 'Course I've always known her as an old woman, but . . .

Carol (*turning to Gavin*) And, Gavin, you—you knew?

Gavin (*quietly*) Yes, I did. But . . .

Carol (*gaping at him*) You knew! Then you can't tell me that it never occurred to you that there is something—at *least*, uncanny—about someone of that age who is so—so active mentally and physically?

Gavin is silent

And yet, this morning, you talked of her as—as someone I ought to be sorry for—a harmless old woman!

Gavin How can we say she isn't harmless?

Carol moves impatiently

And, in any case, when you first told me about your meeting with Lucy, I—I didn't know then that she's as old as it appears, she must be. It was only later when I was talking about her to Grace—why, even the Doctor didn't realize her age—(*to the Doctor*)—did you; not till I told you?

Doctor No.

Carol (*to the Doctor*) And now you do know, aren't *you* going to *do* anything about her?

Doctor (*in a burst*) Damn it, Mrs Clevedon—(*then quickly*)—I'm sorry, I didn't mean to . . .

Carol waves his apology aside as trivial

(*In quiet exasperation*) What do you *expect* me to *do?* Go along to her place and tell her she's lived too long, and then stick a needle in her?

Carol You could tell the police about her.

Doctor (*with more exasperation*) Tell them *what?* That Lucy lives like a pig and grows beautiful flowers and that she's somewhere around a hundred and ten years old? They can't arrest her on that score, you know.

Gavin Carol, you're just talking nonsense.

Carol (*raising her voice a little*) If she's a witch—won't the police deal with her?

Doctor (*growling*) Should've thought it'd have been more a job for the Archbishop of Canterbury or the Salvation Army.

Gavin (*firmly*) Mrs Wilson, I must ask you again: do *you* honestly believe that Lucy has anything to do with your daughter's disappearance?

Mrs Wilson (*floundering*) Well, I—I . . .

Gavin (*pressing on*) When you first came here tonight, was the possibility in your mind then?

Mrs Wilson (*still floundering*) Well, not exactly . . .

Gavin Was it at *all*?

Mrs Wilson Well, no. You see, I knew for definite she'd gone off with a man six months ago, and . . .

Gavin And don't you think that's what she's done this time?

Mrs Wilson (*pathetically, near to tears*) That's just it! I don't *know*, do I —not now?

Gavin You mean since my wife . . .

Mrs Wilson (*not listening*) I don't know, and I don't know whether to let you go to the police. I'm that scared!

Gavin Scared of what?

Mrs Wilson Well . . . (*Wringing her hands*) Oh, dear! Oh, dear!

Gavin (*firmly*) What are you scared of, Mrs Wilson?

Carol (*with anger*) What are you trying to do, Gavin? Just upset Mrs Wilson?

Gavin (*almost snapping*) I'm trying to undo some of the mischief *you've* done!

Carol What?

Gavin Don't forget it was you who put forward the suggestion that Lucy may have—may be holding Doris—by *force* I presume you meant.

Carol (*quietly*) Supernatural force—yes.

Gavin (*at the end of his tether*) For pity's sake!

Carol (*firmly*) Are you prepared to go down there?

Gavin Go where?

Carol *Dark* Lucy's of course. Are you prepared to go there *now*, force her to see you—break into the place if necessary?

Doctor Mrs Clevedon, you can't expect your husband to go down there and start kicking up hell's delight. And why should he? That's a job for the police.

Carol And how long will it be before you get on to them and before they decide to do anything?

Gavin We can't get on to the police without Mrs Wilson's permission. And if she won't give it . . .

Mrs Wilson I don't know what to say. If Dark Lucy has got Doris at her place, and if the police went there, you don't know what she might do to the poor girl.

Gavin On the other hand, if she's nowhere near Lucy's place—as I'm convinced she isn't—but somewhere with a man, then you want her home as soon as possible, don't you?

Act II   41

Mrs Wilson Yes, yes. Of course.
Gavin Then you've got to make up your mind.
Carol (*urgently*) Mrs Wilson, if the old woman has got . . .
Gavin (*suddenly losing his temper completely*) Carol! Will you keep out of this!
Carol What?
Gavin This matter has nothing to do with you whatsoever! (*He moves to the desk and stands with his back to the others. With restraint*) Please, get out of here!

Carol stares at Gavin for quite a while

Carol (*at last; almost to herself*) Nothing to do with me . . . !

Carol suddenly looks quickly at the others, then runs out of the room, slamming the door behind her

Doctor Bit rough on her, weren't you?
Gavin I had to do something. I couldn't let her go on . . .

The telephone rings. Gavin picks up the receiver

(*Into the telephone; in a restrained voice*) The Vicarage—the Vicar speaking . . . Oh, yes, he's here. (*To the Doctor*) It's for you.
Doctor (*quietly*) Don't you think you ought to go to Carol—apologize—make it up with her?
Gavin (*after a moment's pause, moving towards the door, but stopping on the way to speak to Mrs Wilson*) Excuse me a moment, Mrs Wilson. And I'm sorry you . . . (*He moves on abruptly*)

Gavin exits

The Doctor sits on the desk to answer the telephone, his back towards the window, facing slightly away from Mrs Wilson

Mrs Wilson (*as Gavin is going*) Don't you worry, sir. I'm only sorry . . . (*She pulls up with a terrific start—her eyes have fallen on the window*)

The vague form of Dark Lucy is standing outside the window

Mrs Wilson puts her hand to her mouth to stop herself screaming

Dark Lucy hurries away out of sight

Mrs Wilson can only sit gaping towards the window

Doctor (*meanwhile*) Doctor Vann here . . . Oh, yes, Matron? You *will?* Oh, that's fine! Then I can get my patient in tomorrow? . . . Splendid.

Gavin's voice is heard calling off

Gavin (*off; not too anxiously*) Carol, where are you?

Doctor (*into the telephone*) I'll arrange for the ambulance to bring him in ... About what time? ... Right ... I'll see to that ...
Gavin (*off; more distant, and more anxiously*) Carol!
Doctor Thank you, Matron, for ringing me ... No, not at all. I'm very pleased you did ...'Bye.
Gavin (*off; frantically*) CAROL! CAROL!

The Doctor looks towards the door anxiously as he puts down the receiver, then he notices Mrs Wilson's horrified stare towards the window

Doctor What the devil ... ! Mrs Wilson, are you all right?
Gavin (*off; nearer, and wildly*) CAROL!
Mrs Wilson (*suddenly clutching the Doctor's arm*) You mustn't get on to the police, Doctor. (*Her voice breaking*) You mustn't—you mustn't! (*She covers her face with her hands*)

The door bursts open and Gavin comes in in a terribly distressed state

Doctor What ... ?
Gavin Carol—I can't find her. She isn't in the house!

CURTAIN

ACT III

The living-room in Dark Lucy's cottage. Ten to fifteen minutes later
It is an oak-beamed room: the walls, here and there between the beams, are a mellow, rather than a dirty, cream colour. On the floor is a faded but good carpet. A door leading directly to the garden has an old-fashioned latch handle and two sliding bolts, and is flanked on either side by small windows. There is a highly polished, small refectory table laid for a meal for one, with a good deal of cut glass, silver tableware and lace mats. On the table is an oil lamp, which is already lit. A carved, high-backed armchair is placed ready for the dinner. Sacking at the windows is completely covered by long, lined curtains—again faded, but of excellent quality—which fall from pelmets of the same material, placed well above the window tops. The curtains reach down to the floor. There is an antique oak chest, a tapestry-covered chair, and a small but comfortable settee stands before the fire. Below it is an occasional table on which are a silver cigarette box and lighter, cut glass ashtray, etc. On the shelves of a Welsh dresser are good and colourful plates and other pieces of china. The single candlesticks on the mantelpiece are silver, and all the ornaments (including a clock) are of excellent quality and taste. All the furniture is old but of excellent quality. The room gives the immediate impression of being old-fashioned, but bright and utterly charming

When the CURTAIN *rises, Dark Lucy is discovered sitting at the table. She is almost slumped over it, and remains there for quite a while. Then the clock on the mantelpiece chimes eight. A moment or two later Dark Lucy rouses herself, picks up a glass by her side, slowly drains it, then holds it to the lamplight before almost hugging it to her breast*

There is the click of a gate outside the garden door. Dark Lucy stiffens. She looks towards the garden door then, moving fairly quickly, goes to the window and peers cautiously through the curtains. Then she moves almost stealthily to the garden door, unlocks it, and carefully and silently undoes the bolts. She gives a quick look round the room, then moves to the inner door

Dark Lucy *exits by the door below the fireplace, closing it behind her.*
There is a pause, then an almost timid knock is heard at the garden door. Another pause, then the knock is repeated, this time quite loudly, and for longer. After another pause the latch handle is heard to click and seen to move. Then the door slowly opens an inch or two, stops, then is drawn closed again and fairly quickly, though the latching bar is not allowed to fall back into its rest. Another pause, and the door opens again, slowly and wider. Carol, *who now wears a light coat over her cocktail dress, is seen on the threshold. She is obviously very frightened. After a quick look round outside, she steps quickly into the room, and after a quick*

glance to make sure it is empty, she turns and closes the door carefully, making sure the latch falls silently into its socket

With her back still to the room, Carol stiffens as the realization that the room is so different from what she expected—and which, in her anxious state she had not realized at first—now hits her. She spins quickly round and stands with her back to the door. She gives a big gasp as she now takes in the room more fully. She then stands flattened against the door—just gaping. Her head slowly shakes from side to side unbelievingly. At last she leaves the door and moves slowly, nervously and cautiously to the middle of the room and looks round again. Then she goes stealthily to the door below the fireplace, hesitates with her hand up ready to knock, then knocks on the door timidly. After a pause, she knocks more loudly: after another pause she turns the handle and pulls the door. It will not open. She automatically gives it another pull then stands, uncertain, just looking at it. After a moment, with her eyes still on the door, she backs away from it and stands in the middle of the room, nervously biting her lip. She then begins to examine the room more carefully, though all the time on the alert. She looks wonderingly at the dining-table and its lay-out, then at the dresser. She lifts the stopper from the decanter and sniffs it, then replaces it in the decanter. Always on the alert, she goes to the fireplace, stopping now and then to inspect a piece of china or furniture wonderingly. She is inspecting the mantelpiece when she suddenly notices something—a very ordinary lipstick—half-hidden behind an ornament. She picks it up, holding it in the palm of her hand as she looks at it for a moment or two. She then removes the top of the lipstick, and after looking at the vivid colour inside, replaces the top and, almost guiltily, slips the lipstick into her coat pocket. She now moves, with more purpose, to the settee, and begins to lift the seat cushions, searching. She moves to the door above the fireplace and is about to open it, when there is a quite loud and brisk knock at the garden door

Carol gives a violent start, and just manages to clap a hand over her mouth to prevent her scream being heard. She stands quite still for a moment, then moves quickly and silently to the door and carefully slips the top bolt into its socket. The knock is repeated. Again Carol shows alarm. She leans back on the door

The latch is heard and seen to move as the door is tried. Silence. After standing rigid, Carol backs away from the door. Again a knock. Aware that her hands are trembling, she clenches her fists, makes a determined effort, and pulls herself together. She returns to the door, hesitates, then, after quietly unbolting it and hesitating once more, suddenly flings it open and stands back, facing it

> Edward Hastings is standing on the threshold. He is a man of medium height, aged around fifty, with a good head of greying hair and an unusually pale face. He wears a somewhat old-fashioned dark suit, dark shirt and tie, and over his suit a light unbuttoned raincoat. He is bare-headed

Carol (*in surprise and trepidation*) Oh!

Act III

Hastings stands quite still for a moment, just looking at Carol

(*Faintly*) Who . . . ? (*She sways suddenly as if she might faint*)

Hastings, without speaking, moves forward quickly, and catches her in his arms, then after a moment, leads her to the settee, sits her down, sits beside her and takes one of her hands in his two hands and rubs it gently as he looks at her. Carol's head is down as she fights a possible faint

(*At last, raising her head*) Who—who are you?

Hastings, with a smile, puts a finger to his lips, indicating that she isn't to talk yet. Carol, realizing that her hand is in his, withdraws it gently. Hastings looks towards the open door, rises, goes to it, closes it—his back well to Carol. He also masks the door from the audience. After a moment's pause he returns to the settee and stands looking down at Carol, who has hardly been conscious of his move to the door

Hastings (*after a moment, quietly*) Better?

Carol nods her head

Good! (*He removes his coat and places it over a chair, then returns to the settee*) I'm sorry if I frightened you.
Carol It was stupid of me to . . .
Hastings You weren't expecting *me*. (*After a slight pause. With a smile*) I suppose it is rather late for—visitors.
Carol Who are you?
Hastings I want to ask you the same question—when you're feeling better, that is.
Carol I'm all right now. (*She runs a hand across her brow*)
Hastings Now don't move. (*He looks around and sees the drinks on the dresser*) Let's see if we can find . . . (*He sniffs the decanter*) Ah, brandy! (*He pours brandy into two glasses*) Couldn't be better.

Carol, from the settee, watches him absently. Hastings brings the glasses down to the settee. He hands a glass to Carol

Carol (*absently*) Thank you. But do you think we should?
Hastings In an emergency, certainly. (*Raising his glass*) Cheers!
Carol (*with a half smile*) Emergency?

Carol looks at him, vaguely quizzical

Hastings (*with a smile*) I'm feeling a little faint myself. (*He sips the brandy*) After all, I didn't expect to find a—beautiful woman here.
Carol (*quietly, after sipping her brandy*) Who *did* you expect to find?
Hastings Well, Gran, of course.
Carol Gran?
Hastings My grandmother.
Carol (*gaping at him*) "Dark Lucy" is your—your grandmother.
Hastings (*puzzled*) What . . . ? Dark *what* did you say?

Carol Apparently that's what—your grandmother is known as in the village—Dark Lucy.
Hastings (*with a quiet little laugh*) Good Lord! (*He sips his brandy again*) Why "dark" I wonder! Are you here looking after her?
Carol (*quietly*) No, I'm not.
Hastings Oh! Just visiting. (*After a slight pause*) Where is she, by the way?
Carol I don't know.
Hastings You haven't seen her?
Carol No.
Hastings But isn't she in the house?
Carol I don't think so.
Hastings You haven't looked to see?
Carol No.
Hastings But . . . (*He looks at Carol curiously for a moment, then crosses towards the door below the fire*) Is this her bedroom?
Carol I don't know. I've never been here before.

Hastings turns and again looks curiously at her, then is about to take hold of the door handle

(*Quietly*) That door is locked.

Hastings tries the door then just stands looking at it

Hastings H'm! Curious! (*He moves across the room*) You—you don't think anything could have happened to her?
Carol What, for instance?
Hastings Well, she could be lying in there—dead, y'know. God! That's a nasty thought, isn't it?

Carol gives a little gasp and finishes her brandy in a gulp

Very nasty. (*He finishes his brandy*) The sort of thought that calls for another brandy. (*He takes Carol's glass from her and moves with both glasses to the dresser*)
Carol (*as he goes*) Not for . . . (*She is going to say, "Not for me," but pulls up. She sits looking towards the door below the fire*)

Hastings brings the drinks down

Hastings (*holding her drink out to her*) There.
Carol (*taking the glass*) Do you often come here to see your grandmother?
Hastings Good Lord, no! As a matter of fact I—*I've* never been here before, either.
Carol Not?
Hastings No. (*Raising his glass*) Cheers.
Carol (*quietly*) Cheers. (*She drinks—slowly*)
Hastings No. I haven't seen the old girl for—oh—twenty-five years now.
Carol Was she expecting you tonight?
Hastings No. In fact I wouldn't be surprised if she'd forgotten my very existence. No, I . . . I just happened to be in the neighbourhood and thought I'd look her up.

There is a slight pause. Carol sips her brandy

And what about you?
Carol *What* about me?
Hastings Well, what is *your* interest in Gran? You say you're not looking after her. Well—what . . . ? (*Quickly*) Who are you, by the way? Do you live in the village?
Carol I do. My husband's the vicar here.
Hastings (*pulling a face*) Oh!
Carol (*with a half-smile*) Don't sound so depressed. I'm not the typical vicar's wife; at least, I hope not.
Hastings (*coming nearer the settee*) You're not. Believe me, you're not.
Carol (*with another half-smile*) You sound an authority on—vicar's wives.
Hastings Your husband—does he know you've come here?
Carol No.
Hastings (*with a smile*) H'm! (*Moving behind the settee. Quietly.*) Have you been married long?
Carol (*also quietly*) Two years. (*After a little sigh*) Two years.
Hastings I hope your husband still tells you—(*dropping a hand on to Carol's shoulder*)—how lovely you are?

Carol stiffens for a moment while Hastings' hand rests on her shoulder. She gently frees her shoulder by sitting forward and sipping her brandy

Carol He'll think me *very* lovely if I arrive home blind drunk. I think it's about time I went.
Hastings (*moving to the fireplace*) But what about Gran? Aren't you going to wait and see her?
Carol (*rising*) I—er . . .
Hastings That's what you came for, wasn't it—to see her?
Carol Yes.
Hastings Well then?
Carol Well, now *you're* here . . .
Hastings You wanted to see her—privately?
Carol Yes. Actually, I did.
Hastings (*after a look at her*) You know her well?
Carol (*quietly*) I met her for the first time this morning.
Hastings (*with slight surprise*) And you've called to see her *tonight?*
Carol (*looking at him queryingly*) Yes.
Hastings (*half turning to the fireplace*) Obviously, you found her—attractive!
Carol "Attrac . . . ?" (*Looking towards him*) That's rather an odd word to use, surely?
Hastings "Interesting" is what I meant to say.
Carol (*quietly*) She's certainly that.
Hastings (*after a quick look at her*) Look, why not sit down again. I expect the old girl will be back any minute now. (*Smiling meaningly*) And if she *isn't*—it's very cosy in here.

Carol You're not—worried?
Hastings Worried?
Carol By the fact that your grandmother isn't here *now*?
Hastings (*smiling*) I have a one-track mind. At the moment I am only interested—in you.
Carol (*ignoring the implication*) You know, don't you, that she's—old—very old.
Hastings (*with a smile*) I suppose she is.
Carol Very old indeed. (*As a thought strikes her*) That's odd!
Hastings What is?
Carol (*after a slight hesitation*) Doesn't it strike *you* as odd that your grandmother should go out leaving—the lamp burning? I didn't light it. It was alight when I came in. (*Quickly*) And that's another thing! When I came here, that door wasn't locked. (*She indicates the outer door*)
Hastings (*with slight irritation*) What of it, for heaven's sake?
Carol Would she leave the house for any length of time without locking the door, with all these—I imagine—valuable things around?
Hastings Well . . .
Carol (*another thought suddenly strikes her*) By the way didn't it surprise you to see how well the room is furnished?
Hastings Yes, it did.
Carol (*lightly*) You didn't comment on it.
Hastings (*smiling*) You forget, I had a very frightened lady on my hands. (*Moving briskly*) And now . . . ! Can't we forget about—what did you call her—"Dark Lucy"?—and . . . (*He moves towards her slightly*)
Carol (*after a slight pause, deliberately smiling at him*) And—what?
Hastings (*after a look at her; softly*) Well, have another drink to begin with.

Carol gives an acquiescing shrug of the shoulders. Hastings smiles happily

(*Very softly*) Sit down. (*He indicates the settee*)

Carol sits on the settee. Hastings moves up to the dresser, where he pours out two more brandies. Carol, on the settee, looks towards the door below the fire, lost in thought. Hastings, having poured the drinks, moves quietly down to near Carol

(*After holding the drink out for a moment; quietly*) Your drink.
Carol (*with a little start*) What . . . ? Oh. I'm sorry. (*Taking the drink*) Thank you. (*After a slight pause*) You know, I can't help thinking of what you said a little while ago.
Hastings What was that?
Carol That your grandmother might be lying—(*indicating the door*)—in there—dead.
Hastings Good heavens! You didn't think I meant it, did you?
Carol No. But it *is* a possibility—at her age.
Hastings What do you suggest we do? Break the door down?
Carol (*ruminatively*) It would be terrible to think she was in there—dead,

Act III

and we were in here having—(*with a half smile at him*)—well—a rather pleasant time.

Hastings Would you be—more at ease—if I made certain she's not in there?

Carol Much.

Hastings (*after a slight pause*) But if I find her in there—dead, then our—our evening's spoilt.

Carol (*after taking a very small sip of brandy; quietly*) If she is dead, then, I imagine, as her next of kin, you *could* find it necessary to—stay on here for—a while. (*She gives him a knowing smile*)

Hastings (*almost uncontrollably excited by Carol's attitude to him*) I'll —I'll see if I can open a window—break it if need be. I'll go out the back way.

Hastings goes quickly out through the door above the fire, leaving it wide open

Carol (*rising*) But . . . (*She is somewhat taken aback by Hastings' sudden exit. She stands looking vaguely round the room. She gives an involuntary shiver. She then looks towards the open door. She moves slowly up to it and looks through it to the kitchen beyond. After a moment, she moves slowly back into the room. Suddenly she stiffens as a thought strikes her. She spins round, facing the open door—her eyes fixed on a woman's green coat hanging behind it. She gives a little gasp, then almost runs up to the door, quickly takes the coat from the hook and brings it into the room. She examines the coat—almost frantically. After looking at the label on the inside of the coat she feels first in one of the outside pockets, then the other. In the second pocket she finds a screwed-up envelope. Hurriedly she unscrews the envelope and examines it. Being somewhat short-sighted, she has to focus on the envelope. It is obvious from the little gasp she gives, and the expression on her face, that she has made a discovery. She slips the envelope back into the pocket, and, clutching the coat to her, looks around, uncertain what to do. Her hand crosses her brow as she tries to pull herself together. Suddenly coming to a decision, she moves towards the garden door*)

A key is heard turning in the lock of the door below the fire

Carol spins round, putting the coat behind her back

Hastings comes through the door

Hastings (*with a smile*) Boo! (*He turns and closes the door*) No corpse! There was a window open. I got through that. (*Turning again and looking at Carol*) What's the matter?

Carol I—er . . .

Hastings What is it? What are you holding behind your back?

Carol brings the green coat from behind her back

(*After a slight pause*) What have you got there? (*He goes to her and fingers the coat*) Where did that come from?
Carol Sit down, will you? I've got to talk to you—tell you something.

Hastings, after a look at her, sits on the settee

Hastings (*patting the settee*) Won't you . . . ?
Carol (*shaking her head*) This coat—it was hanging behind that door. It—it belongs to a young girl in the village. A girl who is—missing.

Hastings looks at her, surprised

It's true. She's been missing three nights now. Her mother came up to the vicarage this evening to ask my husband's advice—whether she should go to the police or not.
Hastings But what makes you imagine . . . ?
Carol There's no imagining about it. I know this is the girl's coat—the one she was wearing when she left her home three nights ago.
Hastings How can you be certain? It looks an ordinary enough coat. There must be hundreds around just like it.
Carol Apart from the colour. (*Producing the crumpled envelope from the pocket*) I found this in one of the pockets—an old envelope with a shopping list scribbled on the back of it. The envelope is addressed to the girl.
Hastings (*after a slight pause*) May I see it?
Carol (*with a little asperity, as she hands him the envelope*) I'm not making all this up.
Hastings (*taking the envelope*) Of course, you're not, but . . . (*He looks at the envelope*) H'm!
Carol And there's something else.
Hastings What?
Carol (*taking the lipstick from her pocket*) This. I found it on the mantelpiece. I hardly imagine your grandmother's in the habit of using lipstick.
Hastings But what would a young girl be doing here, at Gran's place? It doesn't make sense.
Carol You don't know your grandmother—very well, do you?
Hastings What? No, but . . . (*He unobtrusively puts the envelope in an outside jacket pocket*)
Carol You said yourself you haven't seen her for—at least—twenty-five years.
Hastings No, I haven't, but . . .
Carol Have you any idea just how old she is?
Hastings No, I haven't. I know she must be getting on.
Carol Your grandmother is somewhere around a hundred and ten.
Hastings (*after a slight pause*) That's damned ridiculous.
Carol It may sound it, but it isn't. There are people—*old* people in this village—who can vouch for the fact that your grandmother was an old woman when they were children.
Hastings (*rising and crossing the room; speaking with his back to Carol*)

Act III

But—dammit, if she's that age, how can she possibly look after herself the—(*with a wave of the hand indicating table, etc.*)—well, the way she does? Are you suggesting she's some sort of freak?

Carol (*quietly*) It has been suggested that she's—a witch.

Hastings (*gaping at her*) Is that what they think here in the village?

Carol In certain quarters, yes.

Hastings And do you think so, too?

Carol I've told you; I met her for the first time this morning.

Hastings And what was the impression you got?

Carol (*after a slight pause; with deliberation*) I thought her the most—repulsive and—unwholesome being I've ever had the misfortune to come across.

There is a dead pause. Then Hastings moves up to the dresser and pours himself a brandy

Hastings (*in a subdued voice*) Will you . . . ? (*He indicates the drinks*)

Carol shakes her head. Hastings, with eyes on Carol, unconsciously drains his glass. Having realized what he has done, he hesitates a moment then pours himself another brandy

Carol You're not—hurt—are you, at what I've said?

Hastings About Gran? (*He shrugs his shoulders*) That's the impression you got, so—that's that, isn't it? (*The brandy is just beginning to show effect on him. His voice is becoming a little thicker*) But you can't honestly believe she's—a witch?

Carol Whether she is or not, I want to know what *she* knows about the missing girl.

Hastings (*coming near to Carol*) Well, when she comes back you can ask her, can't you? In the meantime . . . (*He moves to the settee and sits on it, indicating for Carol to sit beside him*)

Carol I think, if you don't mind, I ought to . . .

Hastings (*with a sharp look at her*) To what?

Carol The police ought to know right away about—this coat being here, and see the . . . (*Suddenly remembering*) Oh, the envelope!

Hastings (*vaguely*) What?

Carol The envelope I found. I gave it to you to look at. Can I have it, please?

Hastings (*looking around on the settee*) Where the devil did I . . .

Carol (*quietly*) You put it in your jacket pocket.

Hastings puts his hand in a pocket

No. The other side.

Hastings looks at her quizzically, then feels in his other pocket and produces the envelope

Hastings Observant, aren't you? (*He holds out the envelope*)

Carol Thank you. (*She takes the envelope*)

Hastings' hand closes over hers and holds it

Hastings (*smiling*) You're not, by any chance, a detective, are you?
Carol (*with a half smile*) Nothing so exciting. I've told you what I am.
Hastings (*still holding Carol's hand*) I think you're *very* exciting and—very lovely. (*Almost in a whisper, thickly*) Come and sit down.
Carol (*drawing her hand away*) Considering what I've just found out—(*she indicates the coat*)—I don't think this is *quite* the time for . . .
Hastings (*almost under his breath, in exasperation*) Oh, for God's sake . . . ! (*He drinks again*) You know—(*he gives a little half sneering laugh*)—you're beginning to disillusion me.
Carol Oh?
Hastings If you carry *on* like this, I shall begin to think you are a typical parson's wife after all.
Carol Why?
Hastings They're noted, aren't they, for poking their noses into things that don't concern them?
Carol (*after a look at him*) Good night! (*She begins to move towards the garden door*)
Hastings (*springing up, moving to Carol and taking a hold on her arm*) Why did you *come* here in the first place? To—badger Gran about this girl? Because you don't happen to like the look of Gran you want to cause trouble for her, is that it?
Carol Don't talk nonsense. Isn't it natural I should be concerned about the girl's disappearance?
Hastings Why? Do you know her? (*Nearly shouting*) Does she belong to your bloody knitting class, or something?
Carol (*with restraint*) I don't knit. I can't knit; *and* I've never even seen the girl in my life.

Hastings moves away, drinking

Hastings (*loudly*) Then why can't you forget her for—(*quieter*)—for an hour or so? (*Turning to her, louder*) God knows, I don't suppose you get much opportunity for—for fun in this benighted hole——
Carol What makes you think . . . ?
Hastings (*moving to the fireplace and standing facing it, with his hands on the mantelpiece; overlapping Carol's last speech*) —so why waste the chance when you've got one, and all because of—(*working himself up*)—a stupid little peroxide blonde, who . . . (*He pulls up suddenly. His body tenses. He does not immediately turn to face Carol. He merely stands quite still and taut*)

Carol is also standing still and taut as she stares at Hastings' back. There is a pause. At last, Hastings turns very slowly round, leaving his glass on the mantelpiece. He faces Carol who continues to stare across at him. There is another pause

Carol (*at last; quietly, slowly*) How do you know? Doris . . .

Hastings gives a small involuntary start on hearing the name

Act III

How do you know she's a—a peroxide blonde?

Hastings, after a moment, picks up his glass from the mantelpiece—without taking his eyes off Carol. He then moves up to the dresser and pours more brandy

You were lying, weren't you, when you said this was the first time you'd been here? You're staying here, aren't you? Secretly? Is your grandmother *hiding* you? You know about Doris, don't you? Is that why you don't want me to go to the police? (*A new thought*) Are you—involved with your grandmother in the girl's disappearance?

Hastings has not moved from the dresser. He stands sipping brandy, watching Carol

If you won't tell *me*—(*she crosses to the garden door*)—you can tell the . . . (*She tries to open the door. It will not open. She gives it another tug, then after a quick look at the bolts—which are unbolted—she spins round and stands with her back to the door, facing Hastings*)

Hastings gives her a thin smile, then sips his brandy and puts down the glass. After a moment, Carol almost runs towards the door above the fire, but Hastings gets there first and stands in front of it, facing her

Hastings (*quietly*) Go back.

Carol does not move

Go back.

Carol does not move

(*Quietly, coldly, calmly*) Or do you want me to—hurt you? My hands round your throat . . .
Carol (*gaping at him*) You're mad—you must be.

Hastings gives a wild cry, and for a moment, looks as if he is going to carry out his threat. Carol steps back quickly. Hastings restrains himself with an effort. He is visibly trembling, but never takes his eyes off Carol

Hastings (*moving a step towards Carol; very quietly*) You shouldn't have said that. (*Almost in a whisper*) That's the last thing you should have said!
Carol (*frightened and bewildered*) What . . . ?
Hastings (*almost shouting*) *Why* did you say it?
Carol I—I . . .
Hastings I gave you credit for . . . (*He runs a hand across his brow—with a break in his voice*) I thought you had more—sense than the others.
Carol (*alert, frightened*) The . . . ?

Hastings looks at her intently for a moment

Hastings (*again almost in a whisper*) You thought I meant it, did you—that I'd hurt you?
Carol (*after a slight pause*) No. No, of course I didn't.
Hastings I couldn't hurt you—(*softly*)—you're so lovely.

Carol (*quietly*) Thank you.

Hastings gives her a boyish happy smile

>(*With an attempt at bravado*) Well—can I go now? Please—(*moving to the garden door*)—open this door. (*She turns and looks at Hastings*)

Hastings (*quietly*) I can't let you go—not now; not . . . (*He shakes his head*) You see, you know too much. (*He moves to the door above the fire and closes it*) Doris—she was the same. (*After a look at Carol*) What a pity you came here to find her.

Carol (*now terrified, but managing to control herself*) Listen—please listen to me—and don't think I'm lying, or that I'm making excuses to—get away from here—from you. But I had to make a—an almost superhuman effort to come here tonight. I can't tell you how terrified I was. You see I'm not well; I haven't been for some time. I—I've had a nervous breakdown.

Hastings (*quickly, interested*) *You* have?

Carol I'm not over it. I—I'm still having treatment. When you're in—in the state I am, you get ridiculous ideas in your head—ideas that become obsessions. You won't understand. (*Looking directly at him*) People who are—well, never do. (*After a slight pause*) This girl—Doris—there's no reason on earth why I should worry about her. I don't know her; never met her. I realize it was wrong of me to come here—interfering in something that is no concern of mine. I . . . (*She runs a hand over her brow. She cannot go on*)

Hastings moves to the settee, and sits on it. He has hardly been listening to the latter part of Carol's speech

Hastings (*quietly*) Did they try to—put *you* away?

Carol (*with a start*) What?

Hastings (*thickly*) They did that to me.

Carol stares at him

>(*More loudly, hardly aware of her*) I was as sane as you are. It was nerves with me, too, but they made out I wasn't safe. Safe! I wouldn't have hurt a fly—not then, I wouldn't. (*After a slight pause*) Two years ago I was—shut away. Then one day I had a chance to get free, and I *did*, in spite of that damned fool of a warder who tried to stop me. He tried—but he couldn't do it. (*After a slight pause*) His skull just cracked open.

Carol stifles a cry

>(*Quietly, after a look at her*) I had to do it. You see that, don't you? (*More loudly*) Don't you?

Carol (*with an effort*) Yes, yes, of course I do. (*Bracing herself to say it*) I should have done the same.

Hastings looks at her, smiles, then pats the settee invitingly. Carol, after a moment's hesitation, moves and sits on the settee beside him. Hastings takes her hand

Act III

When—when did this happen?

Hastings looks at her, then holds her hand to his cheek

Does anyone here—know about it?
Hastings (*taking her hand away from his face, and looking directly at her*) You do.
Carol (*with an effort*) And your grandmother? Does she know?
Hastings (*after a slight pause*) When I came here, I had to tell her.
Carol I—I hope she—understood.
Hastings You do, don't you?
Carol (*quietly*) Yes.
Hastings (*urgently*) You mean that?
Carol Of course.

Hastings pats her hand, rises and moves to the dresser and pours another drink. Carol looks quickly to the door below the fire, then the door above the fire, as if contemplating making a bolt for it. She looks towards Hastings and sees he is smiling knowingly at her as he pours a drink

(*Trying to hide her terror*) Aren't you terrified they might find you?
Hastings Who—find me?
Carol The police must be searching the country for you. After all—that warder—you did kill him. (*Quickly*) You *had* to, of course. You and I —understand that, but was it wise to come here—to your grandmother's house? You read of so many people—being caught at their relatives' homes. (*After a moment, puzzled*) I don't remember reading about you in the papers.

Hastings smiles, then, taking his drink with him, moves slightly unsteadily to a small chest of drawers. He opens a drawer and takes out an old pocket wallet. From it he extracts a folded newspaper cutting. He unfolds it, then, after putting the wallet back in the drawer, brings the cutting down to Carol and hands it to her

Hastings (*quietly, with venom*) Read it.
Carol (*taking the cutting*) What . . . ?
Hastings Read it.
Carol Oh, my glasses, my reading glasses; I haven't . . .
Hastings (*holding out his hand for the cutting*) Give it to me.
Carol No, I think I can just manage if I . . . (*She holds the cutting away from herself and reads fairly slowly*) "Mental Home Murder." (*She shudders before reading on*) "No trace has yet been made of Edward Hastings, the patient who escaped from St David's Mental Home, Gorling, Surrey, on Wednesday last, after allegedly attacking and killing Warder Albert Thomas, who tried to prevent the escape. Hastings, pictured below . . ." (*She looks at the cutting for a moment—as if trying to adjust focus. Then, puzzled, to Hastings*) But this—this photograph, it isn't *you?*
Hastings Isn't it? (*He sips his brandy*)

Carol looks at him, bewildered for a moment, then back at the cutting. She sits puzzled. Then she looks at the top corner of the cutting—again adjusts it to focus. After a moment she gives a little gasp

Carol (*almost unbelievingly*) The date of this—November the twelfth, nineteen-forty-*four*! (*She gapes at Hastings*) But—but that's . . .
Hastings Twenty-five years ago. Yes.

Carol can only gape at him in utter bewilderment

Carol Twenty-five . . . And no-one has ever . . . ?
Hastings No-one.
Carol You must be very clever to have given them the slip—all these years.
Hastings (*after sipping his brandy*) I am clever. (*Almost muttering*) Too clever for—that little bitch. (*He fingers the green coat*)
Carol (*quickly*) Dor . . . ? (*She pulls up*)
Hastings And too clever for Gran.

There is a pause. Hastings looks at Carol, and moves to her

(*Quietly*) And attractive though you are, my dear—(*running his hand gently over her hair*)—and you *are* attractive—(*he kisses the top of her head*)—all the same—(*in an almost sad whisper*)—you shouldn't have come here.

Carol sits rigid while Hastings fondles her hair

Carol (*beginning to crack up*) Doris—your grandmother—where . . . ?
Hastings Gran—she wouldn't even listen to me—her own flesh and blood —she was heartless . . . (*He moves towards the armchair by the fire, looking at it intently. He moves slowly and ends up standing directly behind the chair with his hands over the top of it*)

The lights begin to fade

I pleaded with her. (*His hands, fingers splayed, are moving slowly up and down the back of the chair*) But it was no good—I might as well have pleaded with . . .

By this time the stage has darkened completely. Almost at once, a spotlight fades in on the face and shoulders of Lucy Manning who is sitting in the armchair. She is an old woman, untidy, with straggling, unkempt yellowy-white hair. She has a piece of material, which she has been sewing, in one hand, and a pair of scissors in the other. While speaking, she cuts cotton away from the material

Lucy (*before the light fades up; angrily*) No! No, I tell you!

Hastings' voice can be heard close to her, but he cannot be seen

Hastings But, Gran . . .
Lucy I've told you. Now get out.

Hands, Hastings' now appear on Lucy's shoulders, caressingly

(*Sharply*) And take your hands off me!

Act III

Hastings You've got to let me stay here. If you don't, I'll be caught. They'll hang me, or put me back—in that place.
Lucy And that's the best place for you. (*She puts the scissors down on her lap*)

Hastings' hands tighten convulsively on Lucy's shoulders

(*With a little cry of pain*) You're hurting me!
Hastings I can't go back there! Oh, God, if you realized what it was like . . . ! Gran, I'm your own flesh and blood; you've got to help me—please.
Lucy (*fiercely*) I'll have nothing to do with you. I hate you, d'you hear? Hate you—as I hated your mother! Don't talk to me about being my own flesh and blood. My daughter was more my own flesh and blood than you are, and I've never stopped cursing her memory for what she did for me. It's thanks to her that I'm the half-crazy creature I am now. Oh, yes! I have enough of my senses left to realize that. (*After a slight pause*) When it happened—when she came to me that day—my child—my only . . . (*She cannot go on for a moment*)

Hastings' hands move sympathetically on her shoulders

Not sixteen, she wasn't—and told me she was—pregnant——

Carol's voice is heard from the darkness

Carol Oh—God!
Lucy —I thought—I prayed it would be the end of me. For over a year *I* was—put away; you didn't know that, did you? You don't have to tell *me* what those places are like. When they let me out—I was finished—a wreck. I knew that. All I wanted was to get away from people—from everyone I'd ever known—hide myself, and I did. I came here, and I suppose I've found all the peace I'm ever likely to know. I know nobody—speak to nobody—see nobody. (*Angrily*) And I don't want to see—I don't want to see you. I don't want anything to do with you, so get out! Get out of my house, d'you hear?
Hastings Gran, say what you like, I *am* your . . .
Lucy (*shouting*) You're an insane—murdering—*bastard* . . .

Carol's voice is again heard in the darkness

Carol (*in horror*) Oh . . . !
Lucy —*that's* what you are. Get out! *Get out!*

Hastings' hands work convulsively on Lucy's shoulders

Hastings They're not going to put me back in there; they're not! You're going to let me stay—hide here!
Lucy (*shouting*) *No!*
Hastings (*almost talking to himself*) Nobody knows you're my . . . They'd never dream of looking for me here. I've got to stay. I'll be safe here!
Lucy (*shouting*) Get out! D'you hear? *Get out!*

Hastings (*excitedly*) I've got to stay! (*His hands are working convulsively*) I've got to stay—always! (*The hands move up to Lucy's throat*)
Lucy (*suddenly aware of the hands; in panic*) What are you . . . (*With a scream*) What are you . . . (*Her own hands go up, trying to tear Hastings' hands away from her throat*)
Hastings I've got to . . .

The hands tighten on Lucy's throat

Lucy (*in a strangled scream*) Aaaaaah! (*She tears frantically at Hastings' hands for a while, giving choking gasps as she does so*) Aaah!

Carol's voice is heard—in horror

Carol Oh, no—*no!*
Hastings (*in a muffled voice*) I've got to stay here!

Lucy's choking gasps gradually cease. Her hands fall limply from Hastings' hands, which stay at Lucy's throat for quite a while, then slowly slide along the shoulders. Lucy's head slumps down

(*Almost a whisper*) I've got to stay.

For a moment, the hands are raised from Lucy's shoulders and hover uncertainly above them. Then they become tense. After a slight pause, the right hand slowly moves down and picks up the scissors from Lucy's lap. After a moment's hesitation, the left hand moves to Lucy's head, lifts some of the straggling hair, and the scissors, in the right hand, begin to cut it, close to the scalp. Carol's voice is heard—almost a scream

Carol Oh—*God!* Oh, GOD!

The spot begins to fade

Hastings (*almost in triumph*) I'm *going* to stay here—*always!*

The spot fades completely. After a moment, the normal lighting returns. Hastings is standing behind the empty armchair. Carol, her hands covering her face, is standing, shuddering with horror. She gives little half-moans

(*As if in a trance*) Always—always . . . !

Carol uncovers her face and stands gaping at Hastings. There is a slight pause

(*Coming out of his semi-trance and looking towards Carol; quietly*) And I *have*—always.
Carol (*still gaping at him*) "Dark Lucy"—you!

Hastings sobs

You—you killed your grandmother—and took her place?
Hastings Yes.
Carol And you've lived here—ever since!
Hastings In safety—(*looking around the room*)—and in comfort. Gran liked nice things around her—so do I.

Act III

Carol It's incredible—twenty-five years—and no-one has ever known or suspected. (*Suddenly*) Oh, God! Doris! Did she—know?
Hastings (*quietly*) She knew "Dark Lucy" wasn't—"Dark Lucy". (*With meaning*) That was—inevitable. And I paid her—paid her well for her body, and her—silence, but—she was greedy. The more I paid, the more she wanted. She tried blackmail; threatened to let the village know I wasn't a woman. (*After a slight pause*) I couldn't let her do that. (*Looking at Carol, shaking his head sadly*) I can't let—anyone—do that.
Carol (*in a horrified whisper*) Where is she—Doris—now? What have you done to her?
Hastings The front garden—you admired it this morning, didn't you?

Carol stares at him

But the one at the back . . . It's very large, and quite a wilderness . . . (*After a slight pause*) Gran—and Doris . . . (*He gives a shrug of the shoulders*)

Carol looks at him steadily for a moment or two, then moves to the armchair and sits in it

Carol (*steadily*) Gran—and Doris—and now—me.

Hastings, standing quite still, can only look at her unhappily

You *do* intend to kill me, don't you?

After a moment, Hastings crosses to Carol and falls on his knees and buries his head in her lap. Carol looks down at him pityingly

Hastings (*raising his head; brokenly*) Why did you come here? God knows, I've wanted you here—so often . . .
Carol You've . . . ? But—until this morning . . .
Hastings (*shaking his head*) I've often watched you pass down the road. I used to—look out for you—just to see you go by. Then, this morning, when you—you came into the garden—I—I couldn't resist the temptation to—to be near you. (*With a wan smile*) I frightened you, didn't I?

Carol nods her head

I didn't mean to do that. I just wanted to be close to you—just for a moment. But I only frightened you. Then, when I tried to show you how sorry I was, when I brought the flowers . . .
Carol (*in a whisper*) I'm sorry.
Hastings I wouldn't have hurt you for the world.
Carol (*steadily*) But now—you're going to kill me.

Hastings again buries his face in her lap

(*After a moment, quietly and steadily*) But it isn't going to help you, you know—killing me.

Hastings looks up

Carol Doris was often seen—coming here.

Hastings gives a little gasp

    Her mother knew. When the police are told—and they will be, you realize that, don't you?—they're bound to come here, enquiring . . .
Hastings You're lying, aren't you? Saying all this to . . .
Carol To save my own skin? (*After a shake of the head; quietly*) No, I'm not. Because—(*she pauses a moment*)—I won't say I'm not *afraid* of your killing me. I *am*. I'm terrified of the thought of the physical pain—the actual killing, but not of—dying. You see, I've always been unstable. I don't have to tell *you* how nerves can play havoc with your life . . .

Hastings grabs one of her hands and holds it tightly in his two hands

    And I've never been free from the—the fear that one day I might go out of my mind completely, and be . . . (*She pauses*) I'd *rather* die than be—shut away. That's why, always, I . . . (*She sits staring ahead for quite a while*)
Hastings (*at last*) Always you—what?

Carol looks at him for a moment, then puts a hand in her coat pocket and takes out a small bottle

Carol (*holding the bottle in the palm of her hand and showing it to Hastings*)

    If that time should ever come when I'm no longer—myself—I pray God I'll have enough sense—or the instinct—left to . . . (*She weighs the bottle in her hands*) So you see, the thought of death *doesn't* . . . frighten me. I've lived with it in my mind too long for it to do that.

She looks at the bottle for a moment, then slips it back into her pocket. Hastings puts his arms around her and clings to her for a while

    But *you*—will you believe that—whatever your intentions—I want to help you?

Hastings looks at her

    Your life here is finished now. You do realize that, don't you? If you want to get away you'll have to go tonight—now.
Hastings Why should you want to help me?
Carol Can't you *see* why? You and I—we're both—we're both—"possessed of Devils". (*She unconsciously runs a hand over his hair*) But we've—(*quietly*)—no Jesus of Nazareth to—"cast them out". Can't you understand that's why I'm *sorry* for you? Sorry for you, because *I* can understand that it wasn't you—the *real* you responsible for the dreadful—(*she pulls up; quietly*)—for what happened. The real you, I'm sure, is kind—gentle—and . . . (*She cannot go on*)

Hastings rises slowly, moves away, then back to behind Carol, takes her head gently between his two hands, kisses her hair, then, at last, moves away and stands quite still with his back to her. There is a pause

Act III

Hastings (*quietly*) When—you leave here——

Carol looks quickly towards him

—you'll tell the police what you know?
Carol (*also quietly*) I shall tell my husband. I can't deceive him.
Hastings And he'll . . . ?
Carol Gavin will do—what his conscience tells him is right—whatever I might say to him. (*Rising and speaking urgently*) But if you *are* going, why don't you go now?
Hastings (*turning*) It will be easier—(*putting a hand in his pocket*)—when you've—gone. (*He produces a key from his pocket. He holds it out to her, indicating the garden door with an inclination of the head*)
Carol (*coming near him, taking the key*) Thank you. (*She hesitates, looking at him*) I won't say anything for as long as possible—that will give you more time . . . (*She moves away*)

There is a sharp knock at the garden door. They both stiffen, then they slowly look towards each other. The knocking is repeated, louder and longer. Then Gavin's voice is heard off

Gavin (*off*) Please—please open this door!
Carol (*in a relieved whisper*) Gavin! (*Turning to Hastings*) It's my . . . (*After an almost wild look round, urgently to Hastings*) In there! (*Indicating the door below the fire*) Go in there. Lock the door. I won't tell him anything—not now. I'll get him away from here first. I promise you. (*Almost pushing him towards the door*) Please . . .

The urgent knock on the garden door is repeated

After a quick look at Carol, Hastings goes quickly below the fire, closing the door after him

The garden door's latch is rattled

Doctor (*off*) What can we . . . ? We can't break the damn door down.

The knocking continues. Carol, after a look towards the door through which Hastings went, crosses to the garden door and unlocks it

Gavin and the Doctor are outside. Gavin almost rushes in first

Gavin (*half in relief, half in surprise*) Carol! (*He moves quickly to her and takes her in his arms and holds her to him, oblivious of the room*)

The Doctor moves past them, then stops dead as he sees the interior of the room

Doctor (*flabbergasted*) God in . . . !
Gavin (*still holding Carol*) Oh, my darling, I was so scared. I didn't know—I daren't think where you'd gone—what you'd done.
Carol (*quietly*) Were you scared I'd . . . ?

E

Gavin (*with a break in his voice*) Carol . . . (*He holds her tighter*) Why did you come here?
Doctor (*still gaping around*) This is—unbelievable!
Gavin (*vaguely, giving attention to the Doctor*) What . . . ?
Doctor (*with a wave of the hand*) Look!
Gavin (*at last taking in the room*) Good . . . ! (*He stands staring*) She lives amongst all this, and yet—to see her . . . ! It doesn't make any sort of sense. (*Turning to Carol*) But where . . . ? Have you seen her? Isn't she in the house?
Carol (*quietly*) Yes, I've seen her. She's through there. (*She indicates the door below the fire*)
Doctor We'd better get her out; find out . . . (*He moves to the door*)
Carol (*sharply*) No!
Gavin What?
Carol (*hesitantly*) She—she went in there when you knocked at the door. She won't see you. That's why she . . .
Gavin But how did she come to let *you* . . . ?
Carol (*again hesitantly*) The door was unlocked. I—I suppose you might say I forced my way in.
Gavin (*looking at her almost curiously*) You did that? But I thought you were—terrified of her?
Carol I was. That's *why* I made myself do it. I was beginning to realize that if I didn't do something . . . This morning you wanted me to come back here and—and face her, remember? I wouldn't, not then, but tonight—after what Mrs Wilson said—I knew I'd never know another moment's peace unless I found out the truth about her.
Gavin And have you?
Carol (*after a slight pause*) I'm satisfied she's not a witch.
Doctor (*muttering*) Never heard of a witch living like this!
Gavin (*still puzzled*) But, Carol . . .
Carol (*cutting in deliberately*) One thing will please you, Gavin, I'm—not afraid of her any more.
Gavin But what did you say to her? What did she tell you?
Carol I—I . . . (*Her hand goes to her head*) Gavin . . .
Gavin (*pressing on*) What about her age? Is she . . . ? (*With a sudden thought*) And Doris? Did you ask her about Doris?
Carol (*desperately*) I . . .
Gavin (*sharply*) What is it? What's the matter?
Carol Look, when we get home I'll—I'll tell you everything. I . . .
Gavin She isn't here, is she?
Carol (*beginning to show signs of hysteria*) Who?
Gavin Doris, of course.
Carol (*almost wildly*) No, no, she isn't.
Gavin But . . .
Carol (*almost shouting*) Gavin . . . !
Gavin Does Lucy know where Doris is?
Carol (*almost faintly*) When we get home . . .
Gavin But . . .

Act III

The Doctor, who has been listening and is somewhat puzzled by Carol's behaviour, now comes to her

Doctor (*to Gavin; with "jocularity"*) Hey! Hey! Hey! That's enough!
Gavin What . . . ?
Doctor I think you'd better lay off the cross-examination for the time being.
Gavin But, we've got to . . .
Doctor (*overlapping*) I'm speaking as your wife's medical adviser now: not as guest who came to supper and never got it. (*Taking Carol in*) Whatever Carol *can* tell, she'll have to tell the police when we get back.
Carol (*alert*) The police? D'you mean you've . . . ?
Doctor I expect they're at Mrs Wilson's place by now.
Carol (*to Gavin*) You phoned them?
Gavin No, the Doctor . . .
Doctor While your husband was searching for you, I was coping with Mrs Wilson—and as she couldn't make up *her* mind, I made up *mine*.
Carol (*nonplussed*) Oh!

Gavin looks at her curiously

Doctor I saw our local bobby. As luck would have it, his sergeant was there, too. I told 'em about Doris and left 'em to deal with it.
Carol (*hesitantly*) And you told them about—about Lucy?
Doctor About the girl being seen coming here? Naturally.
Carol (*again at a loss*) Oh!

Gavin, after another look at Carol, moves away unobtrusively

They—they'll come here tonight—soon?

Gavin notices the green coat. He gives a start and moves to it

Doctor If you can tell 'em anything—if f'rinstance, you've found out Doris has been here since she left home—they'll be down here like a shot. (*He searches in his pocket for his pipe*)

Carol I—I . . . (*She looks across at Gavin and gives a start*)

Gavin is standing looking at her, a part of the green coat raised in his hand. There is a slight pause

(*Almost in a whisper*) We'd better go
Doctor (*who has not seen Carol's look at Gavin*) Right! I've got my car just down the lane. Gavin? (*To Carol*) And when we've seen the cops—(*smiling*)—d'you think we might still have that salmon? Come on!

The Doctor exits through the garden

Carol Gavin . . .
Gavin (*quietly*) This coat—it is the girl's, isn't it?
Carol Yes.

Gavin (*almost suspiciously*) You *are* going to tell the police what you know about it?
Carol (*quietly*) Of course.

Gavin stands looking at her for a moment

(*Very conscious of the look*) Why are you looking at me like that?
Gavin (*still looking at her curiously*) I don't understand. You seem so—it's almost as if you want to—to *shield* the old woman in some way.
Carol I shall tell the police all I know. I can't do more than that, can I?
Gavin (*after another look at her*) Let's go. (*He moves*)
Carol You go. Give me a minute.
Gavin (*turning*) What?
Carol I want to—to say good-bye to—her. (*She looks towards the door below the fire*)
Gavin But . . .
Carol Incredible as it may seem to you, I—I am sorry for—her. She won't come out of that room while you're here, so please—wait for me outside, by the gate. Please, Gavin.

Gavin still troubled, looks at her, then moves towards the garden door

And, Gavin . . .

Gavin turns

(*Moving to him*) I do love you—so much. (*She puts her arms around him and clings to him for a moment or two, then releases him*)

Gavin looks at her for a moment, then goes out leaving the door open

Carol moves slowly to the garden door and closes it, then, as if utterly exhausted, leans against it, half-turned away from the room

There is a pause. Then the door below the fire slowly opens and Hastings, again dressed as "Dark Lucy", appears in the doorway. He stands quite still, looking towards Carol

Carol has not seen or heard him. After a slight pause she begins to turn slowly then sees Hastings. The sight of him as "Lucy" makes her almost scream with terror, but she manages to stifle the scream with a hand to her mouth

Hastings (*brokenly*) Please—please—don't be—frightened. (*Shaking his head, wildly*) Please—don't. (*He almost staggers to the settee and falls on it*)
Carol (*moving towards him*) I'm sorry, but it brought back—this morning. I . . .

Hastings stretches out a hand and takes one of hers. He cannot speak and is obviously at breaking point

Act III

You—you heard what they said—about the police?

Hastings nods his head

You'll never get away—(*indicating clothes*)—not now—not when I tell them—and I shall have to. You do understand that, don't you?

Again Hastings nods his head

Are you going to try to go?

Hastings (*suddenly breaking down completely*) I don't know—I don't know ... (*Between sobs*) I hardly know what I'm ... My head—it's ... Oh, God! (*Urgently*) Don't leave me! (*He clings to Carol*) Please ... don't leave me!

Carol (*as she gently disengages herself from him*) I must. My husband is waiting for me out there. I must go—*now*.

Hastings (*pleadingly*) Please—please ... !

Carol (*stepping back*) Listen! If you're going you must go as soon as we've gone.

Hastings (*wildly*) Please ... !

Carol (*firmer*) You do understand what I'm saying, don't you?

Hastings (*sobbing*) Don't go. For God's sake, don't leave me. (*He buries his face in his hands*)

Carol (*after looking at him for a moment; firmly*) Look at me! *Look at me!*

Hastings slowly looks up at her

You won't get away—you can't. You realize that, don't you? You're not in a fit state to ...

Hastings (*cutting in*) They'll put me back in ... Oh, God! Don't let them put me back in there. (*Imploringly*) Help me ... ! Help me ... !

Carol Help you? How can I?

Hastings (*quietly*) I'm—afraid of pain. (*After a slight pause*) In your pocket ...

Carol (*not understanding*) What ... ?

Hastings (*in almost a whisper*) In your pocket.

Carol, still not understanding, automatically puts her hands in her coat pockets. She then stiffens, and slowly produces the small bottle. She looks at it in horror, then at Hastings

Carol Oh, God—no! (*She backs a step from Hastings*)
Hastings (*piteously*) Please ...
Carol I can't. I ...

Hastings covers his face with his hands

I ... (*She moves slightly towards the garden door, stops, turns and looks at Hastings again*)

Hastings uncovers his face, looks at Carol pleadingly. Carol, after a moment of hesitation, returns and slowly puts the bottle down on the table beside

Hastings. She then goes to the garden door, and, with hand on the latch, turns

(*Very quietly*) Good—bye.

As Carol opens the door and goes—

the CURTAIN *falls*

FURNITURE AND PROPERTY LIST

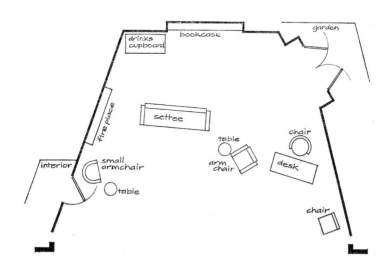

ACT I

Scene 1

On stage: Settee
Desk. *On it:* telephone, writing materials, message pad, unopened letters, paper knife, ashtray, cigarette box, lighter
Desk chair
2 large armchairs
Small armchair
2 occasional tables
Drinks cupboard. *In it:* whiskey, sherry, soda-water, glasses
Bookcase with books
On mantelpiece: ashtray, dressing
In centre of room: Hoover cleaner
Window curtains
Carpet

Off stage: Duster (**Grace**)
Small bag with Bible and Prayer Book inside (**Gavin**)
Cup of tea and saucer (**Grace**)
Bunch of flowers (**"Lucy"**)

Scene 2

Strike: Macintosh and bag

Set: Flower on floor, hidden by window curtain

Off stage: Doctor's bag (**Doctor**)

Personal: **Doctor:** small perfume bottle, pipe, tobacco, matches, watch

ACT II

Set: Empty sherry glass by Doctor's chair

Personal: **Mrs Wilson:** handbag with handkerchief

ACT III

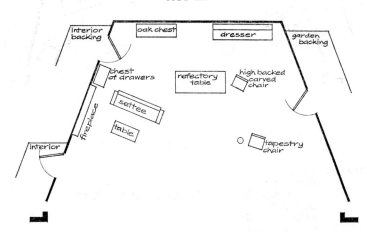

On stage: Settee. *On it:* cushions
Carved, high-backed armchair
Tapestry chair
Other chairs as dressing
Oak chest
Small chest of drawers. *In it:* wallet containing newspaper cutting
Dresser. *On it:* good quality china plates, etc., decanter of brandy, glasses
Occasional table. *On it:* silver cigarette box and lighter, cut-glass ashtray

Refectory table. *On it:* meal set for one, with cut-glass, silver tableware, lace mats, glass of brandy, oil lamp
On mantelpiece: silver candlesticks, clock, good quality ornaments with lipstick hidden behind one
On inside hook of door above fire: green coat with screwed-up envelope in pocket
On windows: sacking next to window, on inside long curtains, pelmets
Carpet and rugs

Personal: **Lucy:** material, scissors
Carol: small bottle
Hastings: key

LIGHTING PLOT

Property fittings required: Act I, wall-brackets; Act III, oil lamp. All practical
   2 interior settings

ACT I, SCENE 1.   Morning
To open: Effect of bright daylight
No cues

ACT I, SCENE 2.   Morning
To open: As Scene 1
No cues

ACT II.   Evening
To open: Fittings on. Dusk outside windows
No cues

ACT III   Evening
To open: Oil lamp lit. General effect of gently lit cosiness
Cue 1   **Hastings:** "... she was heartless ..."   (Page 56)
            Fade to Black-Out, then bring up single spot on tapestry chair
Cue 2   **Carol:** "Oh, God! Oh, God!"   (Page 58)
            Fade spot, then return to opening lighting

EFFECT PLOT

ACT I

SCENE 1

Cue 1	**Gavin:** ". . . record of her in the church" *Telephone rings*	(Page 12)

SCENE 2

No Cues

ACT II

Cue 2	**Gavin:** "But . . ." *Doorbell rings*	(Page 25)
Cue 3	**Gavin:** "I couldn't let her go on." *Telephone rings*	(Page 41)

ACT III

Cue 4	As CURTAIN rises *Clock chimes eight*	(Page 43)